An Explanation of De GAULLE

Books by Robert Aron

AN EXPLANATION OF DE GAULLE

FRANCE REBORN

JESUS OF NAZARETH: THE HIDDEN YEARS

THE VICHY REGIME

AN

EXPLANATION

OF

De GAULLE

by Robert Aron

Translated from the French by
MARIANNE SINCLAIR

HARPER & ROW, PUBLISHERS, NEW YORK

16670

CONTENTS

PART II — De Gaulle and French Politics—Circumstances and Strategy

CHAPTER I — The Circumstances

CHAPTER II — De Gaulle's Strategy

Introduction

To understand a statesman, it is often better to see him when he is not in power. He has less to hide and more time to talk about those things for which he is now willing to take responsibility.

I had four meetings with De Gaulle, both before and after he was in power. These meetings created an impression of De Gaulle which has influenced my way of thinking about him.

The first meeting occurred in 1935, about one year after France was startled to find that she might once again fall into civil war. For the first time in Paris since 1871, Frenchmen had struck down other Frenchmen on February 6, 1934, causing great distress in a country still weakened by the bloodletting of the First World War. Great fear also, for the intellectual and political elite were witnessing the rise of dictatorships of both the extreme right and left, against which the democracies seemed to be doing nothing, mired as they were in their own weaknesses and routines. The young people of the democratic countries saw the initiative in economic and social matters being taken by the dictatorships, and their choice therefore seemed to be limited to either serving capitalistic interests and conservative institutions or adopting totalitarian and thus inhuman solutions.

In the literary *salons*, conversation was increasingly about political questions and less and less about literature. Daniel Halévy, an old friend of Péguy's, with a remarkable ability to inspire new ideas and detect new men of importance and even genius, and a great writer in his own right, gathered together each week in his home near the Pont Neuf, in an atmosphere full of memories of great personalities and events in French life, all who seemed to count among the engagé intellectuals of our country. It was at Halévy's that I met, one Saturday afternoon, a man in whom Halévy felt that the future was already preparing itself, a Lieutenant Colonel de Gaulle. The latter, posted to the Centre des Hautes Études Militaires, had the undisputed reputation of being, with his wife, a regular guest at Marshal Pétain's home and table.

This meeting at Halévy's was in no way accidental, but had been arranged for, on the contrary, over a very long period. After years of relaxation, even pacifism, following the victory of 1918, people were once again beginning to worry about the army and about the way the army was thinking. Was there, among the young officers, a man who could inspire by his intellectual and moral example, in the way that Lyautey had inspired the previous generation? Had the army been able to change its ideas about war, or were the ideas still those of 1914–1918? To get our information we had consulted an old oracle, a retired officer whose career had been interrupted because of his nonconformity and lucidity: Lieutenant Colonel Émile Mayer had had in relation to the 1914–1918 war the same Cassandra role which De Gaulle was to have in the Second World War. Mayer, learning from the example of the Russo-Japanese War, had predicted that bayonet charges, the type of offensive supported at all costs by the French General Staff, would no longer succeed in modern combat conditions, which would instead take the form of a siege and trench war. Similarly, De Gaulle, twenty years later, without any better success, tried to make our military leaders revise their tactics and set up tank divisions. It was Lieutenant Colonel Mayer who had oriented us toward his young comrade De Gaulle, and it was Daniel Halévy who had brought us together.

In the center of the *salon*, which was attended by Gabriel Marcel, Jean Guitton, Denis de Rougemont, Daniel-Rops, Henri Lauga, and many others, a very tall man stood apart from the crowd, not participating in our conversations, a stranger to all the hypotheses which this gathering of intellectuals was putting forward about the future of our country. He was impervious to all these discussions which, despite their subtlety and penetration, would never lead to results early enough to avert disaster. We simply did not carry enough weight.

By the force and immediate relevance of his arguments, De Gaulle took the center of the stage: what France needed was tanks, mobile divisions, a new strategic conception of war which would permit those tanks to break through the enemy's front and cause confusion. In other words, De Gaulle was proposing what the German tanks actually did in May, 1940.

Talk about tanks at Daniel Halévy's? De Gaulle, once more, as so often before events confirmed his predictions, had spoken in vain.

Twenty years later, in 1955, De Gaulle was no longer in power and had not been for nearly ten years. His effort to form a Gaullist political group had been a failure. He was living at Colombey-les-Deux-Églises, where he was writing his memoirs, and from where he came once a week to meet those he wanted to see or those—and they were very few—who wanted to see him. The interviews took place at 5 rue de Solferino, the headquarters of the defunct Gaullist party. In 1945 the office had been full of militants, zealous friends, secretaries, and even clients, and in 1948 it filled once again with those who thought their party was coming back into power. Now the rue de Solferino gave the impression of a resort doctor's office during the off season. I first visited it during that period when one minister followed another, each trying to snuff out the Algerian rebellion. The only person there with De Gaulle was Colonel de Bonneval, whom the Fourth Republic had placed at the disposal of the man who originally set it up.

My book *The Vichy Regime*, written with Georgette Elgey,

had just come out, and since it did not directly involve the General, we had prepared it without consulting him or even sending him a copy. A mutual friend informed me, though, that the General had read it and had said a few kind words about it, and the audience which I requested with the General was very promptly granted.

At the agreed time exactly, Colonel de Bonneval showed me into De Gaulle's office. The General, seated behind his desk, motioned me to a chair. In front of me I saw a mask without expression. It came to life the moment the General began to talk. And what words he used! From the first second I understood what a spell De Gaulle could cast. "Monsieur," he said (and when the General says "Monsieur," one realizes immediately that being a monsieur means very little on his scale, the scale of history), "Monsieur, I've read the book which you neglected to send me." That was all, but it was a welcoming phrase which left you speechless and uncertain whether there was any point in continuing the interview. De Gaulle has a genius for phrases after which nothing more need be said. However, he continued with another sentence delivered in a very Gaullist tone: "Your book is very objective; in fact, so objective that it sometimes ceases to be so."

A year later at another meeting, he disclosed his sarcastic and even vehement rage against the weak ministers of the Fourth Republic who he thought would not be able to hold on to Algeria. "You'll see," he said. "One fine day Hammarskjöld will disembark at Algeria and they'll drop everything into his lap." On this point he was in error: it was De Gaulle himself rather than Hammarskjöld who put an end to French rule in Algeria.

I then heard one of the most extraordinary and revealing sentences of my life. We were talking about the mishandling of politics, especially in our own country, though when I say we were talking I mean that, in the intervals between the haughty delivery of his certainties, occasionally I slipped in a phrase or formulated a hypothesis. "Don't you think, General, that the present confusion in French political life can be traced to the failures of the right in 1934 and the left in 1936 to totally renew our institutions?" Neither sensational nor original, I admit, but hopefully not too inaccurate.

"Monsieur," answered the General, and immediately this word made me fear a catastrophe. "Monsieur, *vous n'y êtes pas*. You are way off. The origins of the present trouble go back to the year . . ." I forget exactly what the year was, but it was an event of the fifteenth or, at the very latest, the sixteenth century. Thus by this surprising diagnosis De Gaulle had linked a contemporary event to a very ancient tradition, forgotten by everyone but himself. He established a cause-and-effect relationship over the centuries which had flown by. He had situated himself in history and dragged behind him, for better or for worse, the uncertain present from which the rest of us had not been able to extricate ourselves.

What extraordinary pretension! Nonetheless it explains why this "contemporary" of Joan of Arc or even Vercingetorix (who battled with Caesar) has so much difficulty in understanding those whom the chance of birth has thrown into the twentieth century, or even more, perhaps, in being understood by them. What are their troubles and sufferings compared to the records of history, spread over a thousand years? "One night in Paris will repair all that," Napoleon is supposed to have said when objections were made to a victory which would cost him the lives of too many men. De Gaulle would have said exactly the same thing!

It is not that he is indifferent, for on several occasions one has seen how moved he can be. But it is easier for him to seem insensitive. To a man who had just lost his mother, he delivered the one banality to fall from his lips in my presence. "One has only one mother," he said, and that day De Gaulle did not address this man as "Monsieur."

Such were my four meetings with De Gaulle, which, all

told, did not exceed two hours. They did not disclose anything sensational, nor were they held at decisive moments in political history. Nonetheless they do provide snapshots which are often more telling than official portraits.

From these sketches five character traits emerge which any biographer of De Gaulle should take into account. The first is his devotion to France, which is his *raison d'être*. It gives him the conviction that he and he alone is chosen to represent and to save his country. The second trait is his isolation, not only from his own period, but from all banal attachments to his colleagues and contemporaries. In consequence he can seem arrogant and even scornful. The third trait is his prescience of the future and disdain for those who think only in terms of the present. Occasionally this makes him seem inhuman, which is only a mask for his intense sensitivity. The fourth trait, his conception of history, provokes the greatest misunderstandings, for the past, the present, and the future are seen from such a height that he cannot understand the more limited conceptions of practically everyone else. And finally, the fifth trait is his very particular conception of truth and objectivity, which are so subordinated to his own purposes that he can often contradict himself without being aware of the contradiction.

All these traits do not indicate a man who is very comfortable or very agile in everyday life. Therefore, for him to have arrived at a position of great power, there had to be a world conflict and national catastrophe.

R.A.

Paris
December, 1965

PART I

THE MAN

CHAPTER I

De Gaulle, 1940 — Adventures and

Exploits of a Newcomer

Charles de Gaulle's rise to power in record time, the way in which he strode onto the stage of French and world history, were altogether unique. In our age of universal revolution, various countries have frequently seen a newcomer reach for power and form a regime. There are many examples, from Lenin to Mussolini, Hitler to Franco, Castro to Ben Bella.

In all other cases, however, these men rose as the result of military or political strategy extended over a long period of time. Even after the revolution of 1905, it took Lenin many more years of doctrinal preparation and agitation to seize power. It took Franco and Ben Bella years of civil war, Mussolini and Castro years of political pressure, and Hitler years of frenzied propaganda and violence.

In De Gaulle's case, everything happened in six weeks. On May 10, 1940, he was still nothing more than a rather obscure colonel at the head of his regiment. On June 18, he was speaking in the name of France. Winston Churchill had known him for only nine days, yet he entrusted him with the leadership of a French government that did not yet exist but which was to sit in London, side by side with kings and other governments in exile.

What an extraordinary adventure! An episode which took

3

place six weeks after the beginning of De Gaulle's rise to power will indicate how very extraordinary it was.

DE GAULLE IS COURT-MARTIALED

On July 30, 1940, seven generals, in command of the "Free Zone" after the signing of the armistice, were detailed to sit on the permanent military tribunal of the 13è Région, which was, in fact, the court-martial then in session at Clermont-Ferrand. Their presence was requested at the tribunal on August 2, at 10 o'clock.

At the appointed time, with military punctuality and in full uniform, they arrived at the Law Courts. The procedure was routine for judging an officer, the tribunal formed according to the regulations which govern trials of colonels, and the jurisdiction claimed by the court in no way exceptional. Only the character of the accused and the nature of the charges brought against him were somewhat out of the ordinary.

General Frère headed the tribunal. Thus, a future member of the Resistance was among the principal actors at a trial in which the accused was to be the leader of the Resistance. Luckily, it was a moment in the war when, under the shadow of defeat, armistice, and the occupation of three-fifths of French territory, most Frenchmen had not yet decided whether to welcome the armistice or to oppose it. The indictment was thus drafted when it was still possible to honor an opponent and give him due credit. It ran:

The retired Infantry Colonel de Gaulle, graduate of the Staff College, has a brilliant service record.

Born in Lille on November 22, 1890, he was admitted to the École Spéciale Militaire [St. Cyr] on September 20, 1909. He joined the army on August 2, 1914, as a lieutenant in the 33rd Infantry Regiment.

Wounded once on August 15, 1914, he rejoined his regiment at the front on October 12. Made acting captain on February 10,

1915, he was wounded a second time on March 10, 1915. He rejoined his regiment on June 16, 1915, and was made a full captain on September 3, 1915.

He fought at Verdun, where he was wounded a third time, and was made prisoner at the Douamont Fort on March 2, 1916.

He returned from Germany on December 3, 1918, and was attached to the Polish army on August 17, 1919. On November 3, 1922, he entered the École Supérieure de Guerre. Promoted to major on September 25, 1927, and lieutenant colonel on December 25, 1933, he was admitted to the Centre des Hautes Études Militaires.

Promoted to colonel on December 25, 1937, he was posted to the command of the Fifth Army tanks, then to provisional command of the Fourth Armored Division. He was made acting brigadier general on June 1, 1940, and under secretary of state at the War and National Defense Ministry on June 5, 1940. He was returned to active duty on June 19, 1940.

He was wounded three times and was mentioned in dispatches four times during the 1914–1918 war. Three of these mentions were in army dispatches and one in a divisional dispatch. His conduct at Verdun was heroic.

He was awarded the Legion of Honor on December 19, 1919, and was made an Officer of the Legion of Honor on December 19, 1934. He also has been given many foreign decorations.

Present circumstances make it impossible to obtain his Bulletin No. 2, but this fact is only submitted for the record. Colonel de Gaulle's position as a retired officer vouches for the fact that he has never been condemned for a military offense.

Thus, it was with an unblemished record of exceptional service that the accused appeared before the court-martial. Or, to be more exact, he did not appear.

As soon as the tribunal had been set up, General Frère announced to his colleagues that, in all likelihood, it would be a trial *in absentia*. In these circumstances, there would be no witnesses, no lawyers, no counsel's speech—only the government prosecutor's indictment. At the opening of the session, the president had ordered the guards to bring in the accused. The bailiff had called out to Colonel de Gaulle in a loud, clear voice, but no one replied; the guards did not move.

Once these useless formalities prescribed by the law were over, everything went on as if the judges, the journalists, the bailiff, the government prosecutor did not know where this remarkable colonel was. He was, of course, in London, at the head of the French government in exile.

DE GAULLE, MISUNDERSTOOD PROPHET

The months of May and June, 1940, which were fatal for France, proved decisive for General de Gaulle.

But in the years preceding 1940, he had not been idle. He had been one of the first officers anywhere to predict the form the next war would take. As early as 1934, in a prophetic book called *Vers l'armée de métier*,* he had suggested "the urgent creation of a mechanized, armored, and maneuverable army for shock warfare. It should be made up of elite troops, and be added to the large units recruited by mobilization. From now on, the fact is that by land, and sea, and in the air, a specially picked body of men making maximum use of their powerful and diverse weapons will have an awesome superiority over massed troops, who will be more or less in disorder."

However, De Gaulle was one of the only highly placed French officers who talked in this fashion. Before the war, the use of independent tank units had not fitted in with the notions of the French General Staff. Marshal Pétain, then the highest military authority, had not believed in their effectiveness. As late as 1938, in a foreword to a book by General Chauvineau, he wrote: "The scarcity of this equipment hampers a frontal attack. The time needed to deploy tanks effectively

* *The Army of the Future* (New York: Lippincott, 1941).

can be used by the enemy to bring up his reserves." In 1934, or the same year that *Vers l'armée de métier* came out, Pétain, then Minister of War in Gaston Doumergue's cabinet, was expounding his faith in the virtues of defensive action before the Army Commission of the Senate. As ill luck would have it, later events were to give the lie precisely to the example he chose to use. He asserted that one need not feel the least anxiety about the Ardennes frontier, for "if we make special arrangements, the Ardennes forests are impenetrable. We can consider them as an obstruction zone. Of course, the edge of the forest on the enemy side will have to be protected by setting up blockhouses there. As such a front would have no depth, the enemy would not be able to press his assault, and even if he were to do so, we would cut him off from the rear. Therefore, that sector is not dangerous." It so happened that it was this very sector the German armor broke through in May, 1940.

General Giraud was another who put no faith in tank warfare. In 1935, De Gaulle commanded the 507th Tank Regiment of the 42nd Infantry Division at Metz. The 42nd and the 45th were the two French divisions maintained on a permanent war footing. His divisional commander was General de la Porte du Theil, and his army corps commander was General Giraud. On military matters, De la Porte du Theil thought well of De Gaulle. In his notes on this regimental commander, he specifically wrote: "Many a brigadier general is promoted who is not worth as much as he." Later, at the time of the postwar purges, General de la Porte du Theil probably attributed his merciful treatment to this early recognition of De Gaulle's worth. General Giraud, however, did not lose a single opportunity to publicly dress down the commander of the 507th Tank Regiment. He did this in terms that surprised, and also irritated, anyone who had to hear them while standing at attention. Giraud's idea was that the only function of tanks was to support the infantry. Advancing on its flanks, and at the same speed, tanks were to help the infantry cross lines of barbed wire and destroy machine guns which held up the advance. De Gaulle disagreed. He believed that tanks should play the part that cavalry had played during the Napoleonic Wars: they should penetrate, advance, and fight in self-contained units in the middle or at the rear of the enemy army.

No man is a prophet in his own country. Though De Gaulle's theories on the use of tanks were ignored in France, they had been very favorably received in Germany. *Vers l'armée de métier* is said to have sold 7,000 copies in Germany, a mere 700 in France. Whatever the truth of these claims, it is certain that the book came to the attention of the men responsible for German rearmament, and that they greatly profited from its lessons. Even Hitler, so the story goes, had it translated for his own use.

In 1934, Philippe Barrès, a press correspondent in Berlin, met Von Ribbentrop at dinner and discussed the French fortifications with him. "We shall cross the Maginot line with tanks," the Foreign Minister of the Third Reich told Barrès. "It is merely a question of numbers and of will power. General Guderian, our Panzer strategist, has proved it, and I believe your best expert agrees with him." "Who is that?" Philippe Barrès asked, probably never even having heard of the existence of a French tank strategist. "Gaulle," Ribbentrop answered, "Major de Gaulle. . . . Can it be true, then, that he is so little known in your country?" "I must admit," Philippe Barrès said at the end of the anecdote, "that until then I had never heard Major de Gaulle's name."

Five months later, again in Berlin, Barrès met Huenstein, who would later become chief of the National Socialist Motorized Corps (N.S.K.K.). "What do you think of our carriers and our tanks?" Huenstein asked him. "Interesting," Philippe Barrès answered noncommittally. But Huenstein persevered. "And what about you? What progress have you made in that field? What is my great French colleague doing?" His great French colleague? Philippe Barrès was puzzled. Seeing his startled look, the German added, "Yes, your expert in motorized infantry, Major de Gaulle."

Philippe Barrès was well versed in the political and military affairs of France. Yet Germans, on two occasions, had to inform him of a name that was well known across the Rhine, but practically unrecognized in France.

In the years immediately before the Second World War, De Gaulle had made great efforts to get his ideas known and put into practice in France. He wrote articles and books, and in 1939 even delivered a series of lectures at the Sorbonne. Military circles finally did begin to notice him, but the fact that he stood for new ideas did nothing to help him gain promotion. In 1936 he had delivered some lectures at the Centre des Hautes Études Militaires, known as the "School for Marshals," but it was not until 1939 that he took command of the tank brigade of the Fifth Army in Lower Alsace.

During all these years he had tried to convince the politicians of the Third Republic. But even though his intelligence and the breadth of his views impressed the best of these men, he rarely achieved anything positive. For instance, he met Léon Blum, the Premier during 1936 and 1937, on two occasions without result.

And so, in 1939, Colonel de Gaulle was still a marginal figure, both by his own choice and in the eyes of the government and the political staff of the Third Republic. The only man he really got along with was Paul Reynaud, who believed in him and would demonstrate it—though by then it would already be too late.

However hard he tried, De Gaulle achieved no real results that might have influenced the course of the war that began in September, 1939. During the "phony war," while there was stagnation at the front, he delivered a warning to the government that was not heeded. It consisted of a few pages, entitled "Mechanized War."

DE GAULLE AS MILITARY LEADER

On May 10, 1940, the German army took the offensive on the Western Front. It first invaded Holland, then Luxembourg, then Belgium. French troops were sent to the support of the Belgian army.

On May 11, Colonel de Gaulle was named acting commander of the Fourth Armored Division, "which, by the way," he wrote in his *Memoirs*, "did not exist."

On May 14, the German army broke the French front at Sedan, piercing through Huntziger's army. Farther to the north, the army of Corap, already in trouble, had to retreat. The Panzer divisions pushed forward through the gap between Namur and Sedan, in the direction of the Oise and the Somme.

The headquarters of the Fourth Armored Division were first established in the immediate vicinity of Paris, at Le Vésinet. On May 15, De Gaulle was summoned to General Headquarters to receive his orders. Major General Doumenc explained them to him: "The High Command wants to establish a defensive front on the Aisne and on the Ailette to block the road to Paris. The Sixth Army, commanded by General Touchon, consisting of units taken from the Eastern Front, is to deploy there. With your division, operating on its own in forward positions in the Laon region, you are to gain the time needed for the Sixth Army to get into position. General Georges, commander in chief of the Northeastern Front, is counting on you to judge what tactics should be used. Anyway, you are directly answerable to him alone. Major Chomel will be responsible for communications."

General Georges then saw the new commander of the

Fourth Division. "Well, De Gaulle," he said to him, "for a long time you have been advocating the tactics the enemy is using. Now is your chance to act."

It had taken six years and a military catastrophe for the French High Command to recognize the value of the tactics advocated by De Gaulle in *Vers l'armée de métier*.

On the evening of the 15th, De Gaulle arrived in Laon, a city startled at discovering itself suddenly in the front line, though still under the dominant mood of the "phony war." De Gaulle found in command an officer who had retreated to Laon with dispersed elements from various units. The Germans were in the area, but no one knew exactly where. De Gaulle, who was himself the whole of his armored division, since not one tank had yet joined him, established his headquarters in the village of Bruyères, about ten kilometers southeast of Laon. It was thus in a village house, threatened by enemy attack, that the prophet of modern warfare prepared to face its reality.

The outlying farmland was rich and lush, studded with copses, dominated by the citadel and the cathedral of Laon. The fields of beetroot and wheat were ripening for harvest after an exceptionally harsh winter. The farm population, used to the false security of the so-called Army Zone in the "phony war," was terrified by nearby gunfire and by the spectacle of mobs of refugees and soldiers. On the evening of May 15, the only reassuring sight was the solitary officer, waiting for his troops to join him before going out to try his destiny.

On the morning of May 16, De Gaulle, still alone, went to reconnoiter. He was probably not unfamiliar with this region, since it was near Camp Sissonne, where, during peacetime, the General Staff had organized countless maneuvers whose futility was now being shown up so clearly. On this solitary walk, De Gaulle planned a realistic strategy—the first such effort made by the French armies in a long time. When he

drew near the edge of the drainage canal that runs from
Attancourt to Sissonne, he was shot at. It was no longer a
matter of *Kriegspiel*; the enemy was on the other bank. He
also came across a few meager French units holding the south
bank of the canal. The canal had swamps along its sides that
tanks could not cross. One could thus defend the area by
merely holding the bridges.

Then De Gaulle saw refugees on the roads, and unarmed
soldiers whose units had been thrown into disorder by the
advance of the enemy tanks. The invaders had ordered them
to throw down their arms and flee to the south, so as not to
clutter up the roads. "We don't have time to take you
prisoner," the Germans had shouted.

"It was on that day," De Gaulle recalls in his *Memoirs*, "it
was at the sight of those bewildered people, of that military
rout, when I heard of the enemy's scornful insolence," that he
determined not to give up a struggle so badly begun. "What I
have been able to do since then, I resolved on that day to
do."

First of all he had to counterattack, as soon as his troops
came up to join him. They arrived, a few at a time. General
Headquarters made it top priority to man De Gaulle's division. On the morning of May 17, the division still consisted
only of two light tank battalions and one B2 tank battalion.
As for the light infantry soldiers, the scout regiment and the
artillery divisions, they were conspicuous by their absence. No
matter. De Gaulle had managed to find a few local batteries
in the area, to which he gave the task of guarding the bridges
that crossed the canal. At dawn this core of a division went on
the attack, through an advancing German army unused to
resistance. The target was Montcornet, on the Serre, twenty
miles away. The occupation of this important network of
roads would hold up the enemy advance. The troops fought
the whole day long in and around this little town, whose
railway station was familiar to all local men who had been

there on leave during the "phony war." But the bombardment of the German artillery, located north of the Serre, and the attacks and strikes of the Stukas prevented the troops from crossing the river. During the battle, De Gaulle was contacted by his light infantry battalion, which he immediately set to work wiping out a pocket near Chivres, and by his scout regiment, the Tenth Cuirassiers, which he set to fight the enemy all night, thus allowing the rest of the division to dig itself into a more protected position. That day, probably for the first time since the beginning of the retreat, French troops had taken prisoners—one hundred and thirty of them. The Germans had suffered heavy losses in men and equipment. The exodus of the local population immediately stopped; some of the unfortunate people spread out along the road decided to go back home.

On the 19th, at dawn, De Gaulle's division took up the offensive again to the north of Laon, in the direction of Crécy. Its objective was the crossing of the Serre, to cut off the enemy from La Fère. The division was still raw, the artillery was ill-assorted, officers did not even know their own men. De Gaulle had only one infantry battalion, transported by buses and thus very vulnerable. His communications system was rudimentary: having no radios, he used motorcyclists or else he went to see his regimental commanders personally. Yet he succeeded in making progress toward his objective. But large German units held the points where the river could be crossed. Their heavy artillery covered the approaches and inflicted severe damage on the French tanks. At last, backed by their own Panzers, self-propelling artillery, mortars mounted in trucks, motorized infantry, and Stukas, the Germans crossed the river.

In the early afternoon, General Georges informed De Gaulle that his mission had been accomplished. Under cover of De Gaulle's counterattack, the Sixth Army had been able to take up its positions. On May 20, fighting their way through a region overrun by German troops, the Fourth Division retreated toward the Aisne to wait for further action.

These two days convinced De Gaulle of the correctness of his tactics, and confirmed his destiny. He earned the rank by which history knows him. On May 25 he was made acting brigadier general. On one of the few victorious battlefields in the French campaign of 1940, the future liberator of France received the rank which would allow him to rally the French and change the future.

On May 27, in front of Abbeville, the Fourth Division was again engaged in mopping up a bridgehead established by the Germans. One morning, at dawn, a young lieutenant on a communications mission asked a tank mechanic the way to the General's headquarters. "The General? He has no headquarters. He's out in the open." "The open sky?" "Yes. Go to the end of the village and cross the orchard to the right, following the hedge. You'll find him over the crest of the hill, under an apple tree." As the officer was moving off, the mechanic called after him, "By the way, if the General has gone somewhere else, look at the ground, going from one apple tree to the next. You'll trace him by the trail of his cigarette butts."

According to Philippe Barrès, who describes this scene,* De Gaulle was then dressed no differently from his mechanic, wearing an old leather jacket without insignia. The communications officer had taken him for a plain soldier and asked him the way. Without identifying himself, De Gaulle obliged him. This probably was one of the last times the General was able to remain incognito.

The fight in front of Abbeville lasted from May 27 to May 29. The armored division had advanced fourteen kilometers and had eliminated three-quarters of the enemy bridgeheads. It had captured five hundred prisoners and a large quantity of

* *Charles De Gaulle* (New York: Doubleday, 1941).

arms and equipment from the Wehrmacht, which had seen its advance temporarily stopped. De Gaulle must have wondered what the outcome of the French campaign would have been had he had under him the armored corps he had demanded for six years rather than a division made up of odds and ends. The future of the world might have been altered, that of his country most of all.

It was a decisive moment for De Gaulle. Now he was set on the track of history. Before this time he had done no more than follow the beaten path.

On June 2 General Weygand mentioned him in dispatches: "An admirable leader, bold and dynamic, who attacked an enemy bridgehead on May 30 and 31,* penetrated five kilometers within its lines, and took several hundred prisoners, along with a large quantity of equipment."

In spite of the fact that Weygand reduced to five kilometers the advance estimated by De Gaulle in his *Memoirs* at fourteen, there was as yet no evidence of the future opposition between the two military leaders.

On the previous day, a curious and revealing episode had taken place. Its source is Captain Nérot, one of De Gaulle's ordnance officers, now a general.

On the morning of June 1, with the division at rest behind the front, De Gaulle informed Nérot that the two of them would spend the day in Paris, where De Gaulle had to make three calls. Since Nérot's family lived at Versailles, he was delighted by this unexpected opportunity to see them.

As soon as they arrived in the capital, De Gaulle was driven to his military tailor, Petitdommange, on the Avenue de la Motte-Picquet. He asked Nérot to wait in the car. Nérot, who watched him enter the shop in a colonel's uniform, saw him emerge, a quarter of an hour later, with the two stars of a

---

* Actually May 27 to May 29, according to De Gaulle, who writes in his *Memoirs* (Vol. 1, p. 38 of the Plon edition), "On May 30 the division was relieved by the 51st."

brigadier general on his shoulder, indicating the promotion of which he had just been informed. "If it's that easy, General," Nérot joked, "couldn't I do like you, and come out a major?"

"You would deserve it, Captain, but I don't advise you to try."

De Gaulle tried out his new rank on the second call, which he paid to Paul Reynaud at the Présidence du Conseil. De Gaulle asked the captain to come back and wait for him there, after making a quick journey to Versailles. An hour and a half later De Gaulle came out and immediately told Nérot of the historic interview that had just taken place. The Prime Minister had asked him to choose between the command of all French tanks or the post of Under Secretary of State for National Defense. The French tanks were so scattered and had suffered such losses that the offer of their command came too late. De Gaulle did not think he could accept. He chose the other alternative, which Reynaud told him would take a few days to confirm.

During the third visit, to General Weygand, then generalissimo, at his headquarters at Montry, De Gaulle and Nérot were warmly received. The Commander in Chief, who so soon thereafter was to become a bitter enemy, kissed De Gaulle on both cheeks and congratulated him in a direct and friendly fashion.

On the morning of June 6, De Gaulle received confirmation of his offer from Reynaud. General Delestraint, a tank officer, had heard it on the radio. He informed De Gaulle that Reynaud had reshuffled his cabinet during the night and had appointed him Under Secretary of State. A few moments later an official telegram reconfirmed the news. Thus did De Gaulle turn from a military leader into a statesman. As Under Secretary of State he was directly responsible to the Prime Minister, who looked after foreign affairs and national defense. De Gaulle had a subordinate but important position in a cabinet that had Pétain as its deputy leader.

The military phase of De Gaulle's career was ending; the political was about to begin.

DE GAULLE AS POLITICIAN

The government which De Gaulle joined was the next to last of the Third Republic and the last to take office formally at the hands of Parliament. Its leader, Paul Reynaud, was one of the most brilliant infighters of political debate. He headed a team made up partly of experienced politicians such as Georges Mandel, Chautemps, and Yvon Delbos, partly of newcomers like Bouthillier, Prouvost, Paul Baudouin, and General de Gaulle.

De Gaulle's appointment was received with very mixed feelings. Those who wanted to continue the struggle at that critical time welcomed him. Churchill, who did not yet know him personally but who had read his book about the career army, was highly pleased by his presence in the government. General Spears, who served as liaison between the French High Command and the British government, expressed his satisfaction in a rather more terse manner: "One of the few European experts in tank tactics. He was for the defense of Brittany, and did not belong to Madame de Portes' circle" (a group, gathered around Paul Reynaud's mistress, consisting of French statesmen who wished to persuade Reynaud to ask for an armistice). *The Times* of London did not conceal its satisfaction. "From the military standpoint, the most interesting change in Paul Reynaud's government is the appointment of General de Gaulle, as assistant to the Minister of National Defence. General de Gaulle has been appointed a few days after brilliant leadership at the head of his armoured division."

There may have been almost unanimous approval of the new Under Secretary of State in England; this was not the case in France, where De Gaulle had up to now always inspired extremely mixed emotions. Although most of the men who met him readily acknowledged his intellectual worth, his outlook and his behavior upset them, sometimes violently. When he was a regimental commander, his subordinates fully recognized his prestige and authority; but they deplored his arrogance and harshness. Rarely was there an officer less loved than he. His disdain and haughtiness everywhere aroused feelings of anger and ill will.

Among the members of the High Command, Pétain, who had once known how to appreciate him and had backed him at the start of his career, and Weygand, who had disliked him, were openly displeased when he joined the government. Weygand would say of him that he was blinded by his own vanity, that he was presumptuous and unbearable, and that his behavior was more typical of a journalist than of an officer. Pétain's judgment was as biting. In June, 1940, he remarked of De Gaulle: "He thinks he knows everything about tanks. His vanity leads him to believe that he knows every secret about the art of war. He could have invented it. I know all about him. He belonged to my staff. . . . Not only is he vain, but he is an ingrate and has few friends in the army."

As soon as he was appointed, De Gaulle said farewell to his division and left for Paris. There he was received by Paul Reynaud, who immediately sent him on a mission to London to discuss the conduct of the war. If Reynaud gave the newcomer such an important part to play, it was because he knew of De Gaulle's militancy, of his opposition to any idea of an armistice. He was counting on the General to reassure France's allies, who were beginning to worry about the mood of defeatism and resignation among some of the French leaders.

THE FIRST TRIP TO LONDON (JUNE 9, 1940)

On the morning of June 9, De Gaulle arrived in London by plane, accompanied by his aide-de-camp, Lieutenant Geoffroy de Courcel, by Roland de Margerie, head of Paul Reynaud's staff, wearing the uniform of a captain, and by the English General Spears, who arranged for concerted action between French G.H.Q. and the London authorities. Spears, who had played a similar role in the First World War, was a Member of Parliament whose love of France was so well known that he was nicknamed the "Member for France." In 1916, as liaison between the left flank of the French armies and the right flank of the British, he had taken Churchill to the top of Vimy Ridge and had introduced him to General Fayolle, who commanded one of the most aggressive army corps, the Thirty-third. "Speaking French without an accent," Winson Churchill wrote of him, "and wearing five wound stripes on his sleeve, he was the ideal person for our delicate relations with France. When Frenchmen and Englishmen have some sort of difficulty that comes between them, and a quarrel starts up, the Frenchman often talks passionately and volubly. On the contrary, the Englishman acts coldly, and even rudely. But Spears had a gift for talking things over with highly-placed French officials, with an ease and a firmness which I have never seen equalled."*

This ease and firmness were to be put to the test during the days following De Gaulle's nomination. Spears at first backed De Gaulle with all his strength, considering him one of England's last chances to influence France. But as time went on, and as De Gaulle showed greater independence from His Majesty's Government, Spears developed a less positive attitude.

On the first of De Gaulle's three journeys between France and England in June, 1940, there was no reason to question the authority and legitimacy of the existing French government which De Gaulle served. It was natural that he go to the French Embassy and be received there by the French ambassador, André Corbin.

At that time there was, quite naturally, great anxiety and

* Winston L. S. Churchill, *Memoirs of the Second World War* (Boston: Houghton Mifflin, 1959).

uncertainty among French officials abroad. What made matters even worse was that communications with France, normally guaranteed by a telephone exchange at Abbeville, had been cut off by the Germans when they took the city on May 19, and that thereafter the Ambassador was often obliged to turn to the British Foreign Office for news of France. The arrival of a member of Reynaud's government, direct from France, was therefore doubly welcome. Unfortunately, the news that De Gaulle and those with him brought was not reassuring. During a private conversation with a French press correspondent in London, Roland de Margerie told him: "'You have no idea of the strength of the defeatist tendency, particularly among the women close to power. I am convinced that our only hope lies in the government's withdrawal to North Africa, along with the air force and the fleet."

Nor did De Gaulle hide the truth of the seriousness of the military situation. "We could not avoid being beaten," he said, "but there were different ways of being beaten." To De Gaulle, these ways excluded defeatism and resignation.

During his brief stay in London, he saw two different types of people. At the Embassy, in the office of the financial attaché, Monick, he saw members of the French missions in England; among them were Jean Monnet and René Pleven. He also saw members of the British government and high command, including Winston Churchill; the Minister of War, Anthony Eden; the First Lord of the Admiralty, Lord Alexander; the Air Minister, Sir Archibald Sinclair; and the Chief of the Imperial General Staff, Sir John Dill.

His meetings with both the Frenchmen in London and the British leaders were to lead to most important consequences in the days to come. At that time an Anglo-French committee headed by Jean Monnet was co-ordinating the purchase of materials. Among its French members were Pleven, Georges-Picot, and Monick; among the English, Lord Vansittart. Set up after war was declared, to compensate for the inadequacy of the Allied air forces, the committee was to negotiate with American industry for the purchase of planes. The members, already united by the urgency of their task, had for the past two years also been drawn together by a common disapproval of the concessions made to Hitler. All of them had been and had remained anti-Munich.

This explained why, from the start, they were so impressed by the new Under Secretary of State, who embodied the will to resist, and why this first contact led them to certain thoughts and schemes which would later be of great importance.

Winston Churchill, among other British leaders, saw De Gaulle for the first time on June 9. He was not unimpressed. He sensed the man's greatness as well as his complexity. One of the aims of the General's trip to London was to persuade the British to transfer their small air squadrons to the French front south of the Loire, in order to back the last French attempts at resistance. Churchill, no longer believing in the possibility of military operations on French soil and from now on thinking only of defending England against an attempted invasion by the Nazis, refused De Gaulle's request, and decided to send only the remaining two divisions he had ready for combat as reinforcements to his allies.

This was proof that England was not giving up the struggle; but it also demonstrated that the strategic union of the two countries could raise doubts. In critical circumstances, the British command reserved the right to determine the nature and the extent of its aid.

In his memoirs, Churchill perhaps confused the dates of his different interviews with De Gaulle, but he remembered very sharply the impression they made on him. He described the General's reaction to his refusal in this way: "De Gaulle then brought up the question of sending to France all the fighter squadrons we had left, for the final battle which seemed a foregone conclusion in every way. I answered him that it could not even be considered. My two visitors got up and went over to the door. When they had reached it, De Gaulle turned round, came forward two or three steps in my direction, and said to me in English, 'I think you are completely right.' I had the impression that, under his impassive and impenetrable attitude, there lay a surprising capacity for grief."*

De Gaulle's first trip to London on June 9 revealed to the British Prime Minister a characteristic of De Gaulle's which is not usually recognized—his sensibility. Outwardly, De Gaulle's mission seemed a failure. In reality, it was the first step in an extraordinary saga.

On June 10 De Gaulle returned to Paris, in time to see the government leave. That very evening it was evacuated from a capital already menaced by the advance of German troops and De Gaulle spent the night in Orléans, where Paul Reynaud also happened to be.

On the morning of June 11 he was on his way again. Before rejoining the government he paid General Huntziger a visit at Arcis-sur-Aube, asking on behalf of Paul Reynaud whether Huntziger would agree to succeed Weygand as generalissimo in order to continue the war in Africa, a plan which Weygand considered utopian. Huntziger accepted in principle.

That evening, General de Gaulle found Paul Reynaud at Briare, at the headquarters of General Weygand, to which Churchill had been invited.

On June 12, General de Gaulle arrived at the castle of Beauvais, the home of M. Le Provost de Launay, where he stayed for two days. He tried in vain to telephone members of the government dispersed among the castles along the Cher, irritated that, because of his rank as Under Secretary, he was not invited to be present at the dramatic Cabinet meeting which was taking place in Cangé.

* Winston L. S. Churchill, *The Second World War* (Boston: Houghton Mifflin, 1953).

When he joined Reynaud on June 14 at Bordeaux, he was told that part of the government supported an armistice, though Paul Reynaud himself still held fast. But the atmosphere at Bordeaux, crawling with political intrigue, was not favorable to further resistance. As soon as De Gaulle saw this, he suggested to the French Prime Minister that he be allowed to return to London to examine, with the British, France's last hopes of continuing the struggle. Two projects were under consideration. The first had to do with what was then called the "Brittany Redoubt," a plan for setting up a defensive front based on Brittany and the English Channel, where the government could remain provisionally and where the troops that had escaped disaster could regroup. From there they could either defend a last piece of national soil against invasion or prepare for a retreat to North Africa.

The other project aimed at insuring the government's and the army's retreat to French overseas possessions across the Mediterranean. France needed English aid for either plan, and especially for an evacuation of troops to North Africa, which could not be undertaken without the British Navy.

These two plans explained both the Under Secretary of State's second trip to London and his stop en route at Rennes, the likely center of the eventual "Brittany Redoubt." Besides this official mission, all evidence suggests that De Gaulle had another idea in mind, which he did not tell to Reynaud, but which was to prove the best one in the end.

The second trip to London (June 14, 1940)

How did De Gaulle come to this other idea?

On June 14, a few hours after his arrival there, De Gaulle again left Bordeaux by road. During the interval he had eaten a hasty dinner at the Hôtel Splendide with Geoffroy de Courcel; Marshal Pétain also happened to be in the same room. Before leaving, De Gaulle silently went over to greet him and the Marshal shook his hand without saying a word. The two men, who had known each other so well many years before, would never meet again. De Gaulle traveled all night. He had with him Lieutenant de Courcel and two or three cars in which were officers of the 4è Bureau de l'armée who were to consult their English counterparts about the availability of English ships for the transport of French troops. In the morning the convoy stopped at Rennes, where De Gaulle went to see General Altmayer, commander of the forces of the West, and General Guitry, the area commander, to study with them the possibility of organizing a defensive action in Brittany.

But the plan for the "Brittany Redoubt" was already compromised. General Brooke, arriving in France on June 12 to take command of the English troops, had had, under orders from his government, a meeting with Generals Weygand and Georges to prepare for the defense of the peninsula. With his French colleagues, he had signed a summary of the meeting which came out in favor of this project. But the moment the session was over, even before returning to his headquarters, Brooke had telephoned the War Office through an English signals system, saying that, actually, he thought the project unrealistic.

De Gaulle's cars left again for Brest. During this last lap of the journey De Gaulle did not even have time to stop to see his mother, who died a month later, on July 16. And so, during those mid-June days, De Gaulle began groping his way to a decision while everything conspired to create an atmosphere of tragedy around him to which family and national causes all contributed. The Wehrmacht had entered Paris the previous day, and in the abandoned capital many episodes, some of them unrecorded until now, showed the anguish of France.

At the American Embassy, four municipal councilors from the Paris area who had not abandoned their posts were received by Ambassador Bullitt, who had been given the task of looking after French interests in the government's absence. As soon as the delegates arrived, Bullitt had them brought in to see him. *"Messieurs les maires,"* he said to them, "in the name of my country, I am proud today to receive this delegation of courageous men who, in the French tradition, have remained at their posts in the service of their people. May I express to you, in the name of my country, all my admiration, and assure you of my devotion to yourselves and to your people. Long live France." One of the visitors, Grisoni, answered with emotion, "Your Excellency, in the name of my country (as we are the respresentatives of the people), I greet you with the same admiration, for I know that you are the public enemy number one of Germany, our common enemy. In the name of my colleagues and of the people, I come to thank you for the moral support you have just offered us. Long live the United States."

When these words had been spoken, the Ambassador took them to see one of his colleagues. As they passed a secretary's office, they saw on the table a little bunch of cornflowers, daisies, and poppies. At this symbol of their flag, the four Frenchmen saluted.

This show of loyalty to France compared favorably with other episodes of that time. The very day after the Occupation of Paris, for instance, one of the most popular dailies, *Le Matin*, came out with nothing but an official German announcement. The proprietor, old Bunau-Varilla, who refused to leave the capital himself, although some of his editors and his staff went to Tours, on June 12 went so far as to rent a suite at the Hôtel de la Gare d'Orsay so that he could spend day and night in his office while waiting on events. On Friday afternoon, June 14, Bunau-Varilla's right-hand man gathered together the few staff members who had not left Paris, and that evening, with a team consisting of an old editor, formerly attached to the Hôtel de Ville, and a young cub reporter,

Bunau-Varilla put his paper to press, the first to appear in occupied Paris, and composed the editorial himself. In the capital, starved of all news, the paper's sale, quite naturally, was phenomenal, amounting to several hundred thousand copies. The story goes that Bunau-Varilla in person counted the takings, stuffed them in sacks, and took them away.

And so, with the Wehrmacht hardly settled in Paris, the two possible faces of France under the Occupation had already shown themselves simultaneously; resistance and dignity on one side, collaboration on the other.

During his journey through Brittany, De Gaulle was unaware of what was taking place in Paris, but as a man who had long foreseen the approach of catastrophe and the course that history would take, he could surely imagine the apocalyptic events which surrounded his mission to London. And it is during this car journey that he spoke to a colonel of a new plan he had conceived, a new possibility he had in mind. The details of this conversation are unknown. It is known, however, that when he reached London, the officer confided to Lieutenant de Courcel: "The General has just spoken to me of a very dangerous plan, which may lead to a court-martial." The colonel was a good prophet.

De Gaulle and those with him sailed from Brest for Plymouth, at 1:00 A.M. on June 15. They reached London at six o'clock the next morning, Sunday, June 16, after a second sleepless night. General de Gaulle's second stay in London was as brief as the first; but it was exceptionally busy.

Very soon the two official reasons for his visit were relegated to the background. Doubtless the officers of the 4è Bureau got in touch with the military attachés at the French Embassy that morning and examined the question of transporting French troops, but De Gaulle did not go with them. His time was taken up by two other projects that he considered more relevant and important. One of these he had confided to the colonel; the other was suggested to him by Monick, Pleven, and Jean Monnet.

Ever since the General's first trip on June 9, the members of the French missions to London had been considering what they could do to prevent military disaster from leading to a break between France and Great Britain. This had led them to work out an unexpected and exceptional plan; its peculiarity was in tune with the exceptional circumstances of the drama now taking place in France.

THE PROJECT FOR AN ANGLO-FRENCH UNION

Monick was the creator of this plan, the inspiration for which he had found in a recently published American book, *Union Now*. In this work the author, Clarence K. Streit, came up with an idea which seemed novel and somewhat shocking; the postwar period, however, would provide opportunities for putting it to use. In order to create an *entente* between nations that would be neither so fragile nor so deceptive as most alliances had been in the past, each of the nations concerned would have to agree to abandon a part of its sovereignty. In this fashion treaties, always liable to be broken, would be replaced by an organic solidarity. Common institutions, responsible for political, economic, or military tasks, would teach the countries in question to work together and to associate on a permanent basis.

Such was the root of a political doctrine which would be applied after the war in the setting up of the Common Market. In June, 1940, the reigning mood of anxiety in London made the English statesmen and De Gaulle adopt this concept which, much later, neither one nor the other was to advocate very fervently.

In 1940, however, Monick and Pleven sought to apply this concept to a plan for Anglo-French Union. In other words, they wanted to confine it to two nations, both undergoing an appalling crisis. This union would have led to such an extensive loss of sovereignty on the part of the two countries that it would actually have involved a genuine coming together.

"The two governments declare that France and Great Britain will no longer be two separate nations in the future, but only one Anglo-French nation. . . . Every French citizen will immediately have the right to British citizenship, and every British subject will become a French citizen. . . ."

The Anglo-French Union would have functioned in time of war through the creation of only one "War Cabinet," and through the fusion of the two Parliaments. "Common organisms must be created for the purpose of defense, foreign policy, finance, and economic affairs. . . ."

This proposal, drafted by the members of the French missions, ended with the call: "And thus we shall win." Considering France's situation at that time, the plan, however adventurous, was perhaps the only hope of preventing France from surrendering.

As soon as De Gaulle arrived, the project was explained to him by Jean Monnet in a little room at the French Embassy. A telephone call from Bordeaux by Paul Reynaud had informed the General that since his departure the situation had grown still worse, and that Reynaud was under terrible pressure to agree to an armistice and was on the point of resigning. Quick action was imperative.

De Gaulle immediately agreed to the plan for an Anglo-French Union, and that same morning he telephoned Paul Reynaud from Monnet's office to outline the plan and to give him a general picture of the new idea. Perhaps this telephone call might act as the life buoy that the French Prime Minister needed in order to hold out.

Later that morning at the Embassy, De Gaulle performed one of the few executive acts of his very short stay in power in the Reynaud government. The French ship Pasteur was to bring to France from the United States a thousand 75 mm. cannons, thousands of machine guns, and large amounts of munitions. Its original destination had been Bordeaux. To avoid the risk of letting this priceless cargo fall into the hands of the enemy, De Gaulle had the *Pasteur* change course. He ordered it to make for a British port.

Then, at the Carlton Club, the French Under Secretary of State, accompanied by Ambassador Corbin and Jean Monnet, met the British Prime Minister for lunch. Paul Reynaud's critical situation dominated the conversation. Churchill first asked about the French fleet—it was essential for the further conduct of the war that it should not be surrendered to the Germans under any circumstances. On this point De Gaulle reassured him, but the near future would soon reveal that he himself did not wholly believe his own assurances. Then the question of the union came up. De Gaulle described it to Churchill, who had already been informed of it by Lord Halifax. "But it's quite a mouthful," Churchill said at first. Mouthful or not, it was the only chance then remaining. The decision had to be made at once. A possibly decisive French Cabinet meeting was to be held in Bordeaux at five o'clock that afternoon.

Churchill immediately summoned the British Cabinet to Downing Street and returned there himself with De Gaulle and Ambassador Corbin. De Gaulle kept Paul Reynaud informed by telephone.

This Cabinet meeting lasted two hours, during which time De Gaulle and Corbin stayed in an office next door to the Cabinet room. Although they were of course unable to know the details of the meeting, they could sense the direction it was taking from the comings and goings of some of the ministers, who left their colleagues to come in and ask them for detailed advice on certain points. One can imagine the anxiety of the two Frenchmen, thinking that their country's fate was being decided on the other side of the wall.

Suddenly, the entire British Cabinet, headed by Churchill, came out of the conference room. It was the crucial moment. "We agree," Churchill said.

At the same moment in Bordeaux, in the temporary offices

of the French Prime Minister, a dramatic scene was taking place that fully showed the desperate situation in which Paul Reynaud's government found itself. The French Prime Minister had summoned the British Ambassador, Sir Ronald Campbell, and General Spears to inform them of the contents of an appeal which he intended to send to President Roosevelt. In the text he had composed, which he showed to the two Englishmen, he said, "If the United States does not enter the war immediately, France will be forced to capitulate, and England will soon follow." On reading this, Spears gave a start. "You have no right to send this telegram," he said. "You can speak for yourself but not for us." And he tore up the draft.

The pieces were floating down onto a table of imitation ebony, which separated the two speakers, at the exact moment that the telephone rang. It was De Gaulle calling Paul Reynaud from London to tell him of the British decision and to give him the text of the proposed union acceptable to His Majesty's Government.

Paul Reynaud, writing with a gold pencil, took down the text under dictation, repeating every word aloud so that Campbell and Spears immediately knew what it was about. The amazed Spears, forgetting the previous scene, held the paper for Reynaud, who, because he had the receiver in his left hand and the pencil in his right, could not keep the paper steady himself.

When Paul Reynaud had finished this exercise—suited to school children rather than to heads of government—he asked in French over the telephone: "Does *he* agree?" There was a silence. Then the listeners could guess that the speakers at the other end of the line had changed, for Reynaud now switched to English. The "he" was, of course, Churchill, to whom De Gaulle had passed the receiver so that he could personally confirm his support of the plan.

"Hello? Reynaud?" Churchill said. "De Gaulle is right.

Our proposal can have great results. You must hold out." Then, after listening to Paul Reynaud's reply, he said, "All right, until tomorrow then, at Concarneau." In Bordeaux, Reynaud hung up and said to Spears, "Now our government will certainly agree." Spears did not hide his joy.

That same evening, at Waterloo Station, accompanied by the leaders of the Liberal and the Labor parties, by his General Staff, and by a number of top officials, Churchill boarded a special train that was to take him to Southampton, where he would sail to reach Concarneau on the following day, June 17, at noon. His wife came to say good-by, but in spite of the fact that all the travelers were aboard, the train did not start. Something was wrong. Suddenly Churchill's personal secretary arrived, out of breath. He had come directly from Downing Street to the platform, bringing a message sent from Bordeaux by Ambassador Campbell: "Open crisis in French government. . . . Hope to have news towards midnight. Meanwhile, meeting arranged for tomorrow impossible."

Had something happened at Bordeaux round that table of imitation ebony?

The dictation was hardly over, the receiver hardly hung up, before Spears, anticipating the signing of the Anglo-French Union and already considering himself Paul Reynaud's right hand, took the piece of paper into a nearby office. He handed the historic document to a secretary and asked her to copy it.

It was not only a declaration of intention, but also a precise plan for conducting the war:

The two nations will be responsible for war reparations, wherever they are incurred, and the resources of both countries will be used for this purpose equally, and as if forming one whole.

For the duration of the war, there will be only one War Cabinet, and all the forces of Great Britain and France, by land, sea, or air, will be placed under its direction.

The War Cabinet will be located wherever it decides it can govern most efficiently. The two Parliaments will officially merge. The dominions which form the British Empire are already recruiting new armies. France will maintain its available forces on land, sea, and air. The union calls on the United States, and asks it to reinforce the economy of the Allies, and to bring the aid of its powerful resources to the common cause.

The union will concentrate all its energies against the enemy's strength, wherever the struggle is waged.

And thus we shall win.

At this very same time in London, Lieutenant de Courcel, who was waiting at the Embassy for the results of the British Cabinet meeting, saw De Gaulle rushing back from Downing Street at full speed. "We're leaving right away for Bordeaux, in a plane put at our disposal by Churchill." And so De Gaulle, Lieutenant de Courcel, and some of the officers from the 4è Bureau took the plane back to France. During this brief stay in London, De Gaulle had left the mission with which he had been entrusted in the hands of his subordinates, and had concentrated instead on the plan of Jean Monnet, Monick, and Pleven for a union. In all likelihood he had also had private conferences with Churchill about the secret project which he had talked over with the Colonel on the journey over.

His departure from the airport took place on June 16. On landing, the General learned that he was no longer Under Secretary of State. Two members of his staff, Colonels Himbert and Auburtin, had come to inform him of what had taken place since his telephone call.

Reynaud had not succeeded in getting the plan for the Anglo-French Union adopted by his Cabinet. Only six members of his government—Mandel, Campinchi, Louis Marin, Dautry, Rio, and Georges Monnet—had backed him. Seventeen others, among them Marshal Pétain, Bouthillier, Pernot, Frossard, Yvon Delbos, Chichery, Chautemps, and Laurent-Eynac, had not believed that they could give the plan their support. Paul Reynaud had promptly resigned. He would be replaced immediately by Marshal Pétain.

De Gaulle foresaw at once the fatal consequences of the change-over: the new government would ask for an armistice.

As soon as they arrived in Bordeaux proper, De Gaulle and De Courcel went to a little hotel near the Splendide. It was on a street that ran at right angles from the Splendide's façade. In these commonplace rooms, found by luck in the overcrowded town, the two men spent their last night in France before their victorious return in 1944.

De Gaulle's last hours in France (June 16 and 17, 1940)

Before supper, De Gaulle went to see Paul Reynaud, whose resignation, though accepted, was not yet official. De Gaulle informed him that he was leaving for London again the next morning. From there he would attempt to restore morale and regroup the nucleus of a French force. To help him establish the minimum organization necessary in London, Reynaud had one hundred thousand francs transferred to De Gaulle from secret funds. To facilitate his departure, he signed an order sending the General on a mission, still in his capacity as Under Secretary of State. To De Courcel, De Gaulle summarized the impression made on him by Reynaud: "I saw a man who had been discharged, and who felt relieved." De Gaulle and De Courcel then had dinner at the Splendide, and after the meal went to the rue Vital-Carles, where the Cabinet offices were located. There they met the British Ambassador and also General Spears, whose destiny, for a time, joined with that of De Gaulle and Lieutenant de Courcel.

Indeed, Spears was to be the witness and companion of their departure for England and their installation in London. He was to share in their fortunes. But the historian must note and regret the fact that these men, living through one of history's great moments, witnessing and participating in the same events, should yet have preserved such different recollections of them. The suspicion arises that each is claiming for himself the responsibility for the escape.

According to General Spears, De Gaulle, during that evening of June 16, did not want to be seen or to draw too much attention to himself. He feared arrest, a possibility which was far from unlikely in Bordeaux after Reynaud's resignation. (On the following day, in fact, Georges Mandel, his colleague in government, was arrested at lunchtime.) In the hallway at the rue Vital-Carles Spears saw the General leaning back against a column, concealing himself behind it so that he would not be seen from the entrance. He was very pale, and insisted that he had good reason to believe Weygand wanted his arrest. Knowing that an English ship, the destroyer H.M.S. *Berkeley*, had dropped anchor in the estuary of the Gironde, he asked to spend the night there (a plan which De Gaulle and De Courcel said they never even considered). It was the only place in Bordeaux where he would be safe.

It was difficult to have a conversation of this kind in a hallway. The two Englishmen and the two Frenchmen therefore went to the Hôtel Montré, where Campbell and Spears were staying. In the Ambassador's room, De Gaulle again voiced his fears. At the same time, he stressed his determination to do everything in his power to reach England the next day. The French Empire's fate was at stake. The call for French resistance could only be launched from London, before the Bordeaux government decided on an irrevocable armistice. If North Africa and the French Empire were still to be saved, this too could only be done from England. Thus the immediate problem for him was to avoid arrest and to reach England.

The English plane which had brought him back from London that very evening remained at his disposal. According to Spears, the order to fly depended on himself. According to

De Gaulle and De Courcel, it depended on them. But isn't the argument academic, since all three had agreed that they would leave for London the next day?

According to Spears, where De Gaulle spent his last night in France remains unknown. This mystery fits in with his interpretation of De Gaulle as suffering from strain and a very violent emotional shock on his arrival in Bordeaux. According to De Courcel, the General and he, after leaving the Hôtel Montré, simply returned to their little hotel not far from the Splendide. There they spent a peaceful night, in rooms that they had rented upon their arrival.

Very early the next morning De Gaulle began to receive his collaborators at his hotel. The farewells of the dismissed Minister to the members of his staff hardly conformed to protocol. He made appointments for the afternoon with some of them, in order, apparently, not to arouse suspicions about his plans for fleeing.

When he had finished with them, he told De Courcel: "I'm leaving for London in an hour. Have my luggage ready. What do you want to do?" "I don't want to remain in France," the lieutenant replied. "In that case, come with me." Lieutenant de Courcel then asked the General if there would be any room for him on the plane. De Gaulle answered that there would be room, as he was the only one leaving. The other officers had relatives in France, and wanted to wait for news of them before going to London. In fact, not one of them left for London that day, but later several of them reached England or joined the Resistance in France.

And so, the English plane could count on two passengers for its return flight. At the same time a third passenger, Spears, was also getting his luggage ready. On the previous evening he had asked to telephone London from his room at the Hôtel Montré. When he heard Churchill's voice speaking to him from across the Channel and across occupied territory in France, Spears told him of his despair at what was taking place in France, and said he was returning. At the same time, he asked permission to bring De Gaulle back with him.

THE THIRD JOURNEY TO LONDON (JUNE 17, 1940)

The next morning at the airport, the discrepancies between the accounts of De Gaulle and De Courcel and of General Spears begin again. According to Spears, De Gaulle was still obsessed by the fear of being arrested. For this reason, he wanted to mislead others about his real intentions.

Once they reached the airfield, the travelers saw an unforgettable sight. The ground in front of the hangars was covered with planes, almost wing to wing, stretching out as far as the eye could see. Spears could not remember ever seeing so many. It was obvious that all the planes able to fly were gathered there in case of a flight to North Africa.

This mass of machines, leaving no space free, worried the pilot, who was not sure that he would find enough room to take off. The stowing away of the General's heavy luggage also had to be done discreetly.

At last everything was ready. Spears climbed aboard as though he were the only one leaving French soil. De Gaulle remained near the plane, as if intending to salute its departure. The motor started up, the propellers began turning, Spears said good-by to his French chauffeur. The plane began to move, but before it had gathered speed, Spears leaned out of the cockpit and stretched his hands toward the General, who caught them. He heaved De Gaulle on board. It was a genuine kidnaping. De Courcel, more agile, made a dash and was inside the plane in two seconds. The hatch slid shut and the plane took off. Spears opened that day's newspaper from the southwest of France. While the plane rose higher, carrying, in Churchill's words, France's honor in its bowels, Spears read aloud an article in praise of his traveling companion. This was probably the last article in any newspaper officially published in Occupied France to praise De Gaulle.

According to Spears, these are the details of the departure. As soon as the plane had taken off, he began to write his notes. Today this enables him to maintain his version against that of everyone else. He declares that De Gaulle in effect played the role of a stowaway.

In his *Memoirs*,* General de Gaulle makes a scornful reference to his British partner's account. "The departure," he writes, "took place without romanticism and without complication."

Lieutenant de Courcel, later French Ambassador in London, supplies details which contradict General Spears' narrative. De Gaulle, he claims, had no reason to hide himself, since he was within his rights and was leaving for London on a regular mission. De Courcel claims to prove his case by telling of his meeting with two members of Paul Reynaud's staff on the airfield. When they asked what he was doing there, De Courcel answered, "We are leaving for England, to find the ships needed for the transport of our French troops."

After twenty-five years, it is difficult for the historian to serve as arbiter in a dispute of this nature. Experience teaches one thing, however, and that is that during days as dramatic as those of June, 1940, recollections become telescoped in human memory; they take on different colors, depending on the later positions of the actors or witnesses in such a drama. And even if facts are recorded correctly, their interpretation usually varies.

General de Gaulle and Ambassador de Courcel have kindly written to me to uphold their points of view, and General Spears has done the same. The question is still unresolved, since each one sticks to his version.

Whatever the circumstances, the fact is that the plane took off, made for the Atlantic between Oléron and Lapalisse, flew over the *Champlain*, which was sinking, and crossed Brittany, passing over Paimpont, where the General's mother

* *The Complete War Memoirs of Charles de Gaulle* (New York: Simon and Schuster, 1959).

lived (in the outlying districts of that town, munitions depots were exploding in the smoke-filled forests).

The plane made a stop in Jersey to refuel. The Germans would occupy the island eleven days later. It was cold; the airport was abandoned except for a very pretty woman serving at the canteen. Finding himself on British territory again, Spears played host to De Gaulle, asking him what he wanted. The General wanted a cup of coffee; but he found that the liquid in the container handed him by Spears had a queer taste. "I don't want to criticize you," the General told Spears, "but truth compels me to tell you that this is not coffee. It is tea." "Indeed," General Spears concludes in his book on these events, "this was De Gaulle's first contact with the lukewarm liquid which replaces all others in England . . . his martyrdom had begun."

The plane landed at the airport of Heston, near London, toward the middle of the day. The weather was still fine. Spears invited his traveling companions to lunch. That afternoon De Gaulle made a round of calls, but this time he did not go to the French Embassy. His life as a rebel and a dissenter had begun.

De Gaulle the dissenter

After lunch at the Royal Automobile Club, General de Gaulle went to see Churchill, whom he found enjoying the sunshine in the garden of Downing Street. They came to an agreement which authorized De Gaulle to launch a preliminary appeal on the radio. After that he went with De Courcel to 6 Seymour Place, near Hyde Park. Before they left Bordeaux, they had been given the key to a small bachelor apartment belonging to Jean Laurent, of the Bank of Indochina, who had taken part in a French financial mission to London during the "phony war." During his brief period in power in France, De Gaulle had appointed Laurent director of his staff, and Laurent, unable to leave France, had handed De Gaulle the key to his apartment along with the 100,000 francs that Reynaud had given him from secret funds.

That afternoon, De Gaulle and De Courcel settled in. De Courcel went to change Paul Reynaud's travel money at the Bank of England; this was how the first war treasury of the Free French was established. Lieutenant de Courcel spent it sparingly, penny by penny, until Pierre Dennis took over the nucleus of the Gaullist finances. Later Dennis described the beginnings of his important duties in the following picturesque terms:

I clearly remember the incidents of my installation in office. In accordance with the General's instructions, I went down the corridor and opened a door, on which the word *Caisse* was written in a sergeant major's round handwriting. I came into a small triangular room, with a window facing the Thames. There I found an old man with a grave, emaciated face, sitting at a rickety table. He and I held the first technical conversation concerning Free France's financial situation. It turned out that, on the previous day, there had still been fourteen shillings in the till, but that this had run out during the day. He had had to put in ten shillings out of his own pocket to pay for two telegrams that the General, in his lack of consideration for our limited means of action, had thought it useful to send. We did not have an account anywhere, nor, as far as he knew, was there anyone who would give us credit. He himself had just come from France, and felt out of his element. He had not yet had the opportunity to check if there were any banks in England.

This description of what took place a few days after the General's arrival indicates not only how insubstantial the finances were but how uncoordinated were the skeleton staffs in the first offices. However, by this time Free France at least had premises, and a sergeant major's round handwriting at its disposal, for when they first arrived on June 17, neither De Gaulle nor De Courcel had yet acquired such refinements.

After his visit to Winston Churchill, De Gaulle returned to Seymour Place and spent the afternoon composing his speech in Jean Laurent's apartment. Once written it had to be typed, but the two newcomers obviously did not yet have a secretariat. Fortunately De Courcel remembered that a friend of his family, Elisabeth de Miribel, was working for a French mission in London and he asked her to come over and type out the speech.

On the evening of the 17th, De Gaulle and De Courcel went to have dinner at Jean Monnet's home. René Pleven was there. Mme. Monnet remembers hearing De Gaulle explain why he did not want to read his appeal over the B.B.C. that evening. The request for an armistice had not yet been made official, and his speech could influence the troops which were still fighting. And so he would wait until the following day.

The next day, June 18, at six o'clock, the General read his appeal from a B.B.C. studio while Spears and De Courcel listened in an adjoining room. This famous text is sometimes confused with a poster that appeared on the walls of London during August ("France has lost a battle, but it has not lost the war"). The speech consisted only of an appeal for military resistance, and had no bearing on politics. De Gaulle spoke as a war leader, not as the head of a government.

"I, General de Gaulle, at present in London, call on the French officers and soldiers who find themselves on British territory or who may arrive there, with or without their arms, I call on the engineers and the skilled workers in the armament industries who find themselves on British territory or who may arrive there, to get in contact with me."

DE GAULLE ACTS AS SPOKESMAN FOR FRANCE

The very day after this appeal, volunteers came forward. For lack of a better spot, the General received them in his apartment at Seymour Place. The following description of the beginnings of the Free French is by one of De Gaulle's first visitors, Pierre Bourdan:

We came into a light, impersonal hallway, leading to a corridor which ran the length of the house. A vast bay window filled the whole corridor with sunlight. We waited a few minutes. The General was holding a meeting with a group of Frenchmen, among them Denis Saurat, Director of the French Institute in London. . . . Along the corridor, seven or eight men were talking in whispers. A tall, slender cavalry lieutenant with light eyes, a large nose, and courteous manners asked for our names and told us his was De Courcel. Without any other formalities he ushered us into a huge, comfortably furnished office, as impersonal as the rest of the apartment, where we found General de Gaulle.*

Bourdan also recorded his impressions of the unknown general who met visitors so casually in his role as the only military hope left to France.

I saw a man from another age. Very tall, he was wearing a uniform and leggings and held himself extremely straight. But this erectness, accentuated by his thrown-back head and by his arms, which followed exactly the line of his body, seemed a natural and comfortable position for him. . . . The bearing of his head, so very remote, and the expression of his face showed his intransigence. At first his features reminded me of a medieval drawing. I felt like framing them with a visor and a chinpiece. There was something aquiline and unchanging about the eyes and the shape of the eyelids. But a touch of awkwardness was added to the face by the very long and bulbous nose. . . . The chief characteristic of his eyes was that they were oblivious of the outer world. Their expression could not change to suit the mood of the people around him. Their look seemed preordained.†

On June 19, De Gaulle settled down to his new situation. Physically, he moved into a more appropriate and convenient location than Seymour Place. General Spears, who had an

---

* Pierre Bourdan, *Cornet des jours d'attente* (Paris: Trémois, 1945).
† *Ibid.*

office at St. Stephen's, a stone's throw from Big Ben, thought of asking his doorkeeper if there was an empty floor in the blackened brick building. When he found that there was, he informed De Gaulle, who moved in the nucleus of his staff the very next day.

Politically, June 19th represents a decisive change of attitude on the General's part. This change has not been pointed out frequently enough. His B.B.C. speech of the previous day had been that of a military leader. On the 19th, using the microphone for a second time, he spoke as a political leader and as a statesman. It was on that day that he finally broke off relations with Pétain's government:

"At the present hour, all Frenchmen understand that the usual forms of government have disappeared.

"Confronted with the confusion of French souls, confronted with the liquidation of a government which has fallen under the yoke of the enemy, confronted with the fact that our institutions cannot function freely, I, General de Gaulle, French soldier and leader, am aware of speaking in the name of France."

The reason for such a change in attitude has not been pointed out. It came as the result of a quick trip to France by four members of the French missions in London—Monnet, Pleven, Monick, and Marjolin—though the idea for this trip had come from the French Ambassador, André Corbin. The four experts knew some of the ministers who had just become members of Marshal Pétain's government. These men would be responsible for the signing of an armistice or the continuation of the war from British shores. Thus a last attempt could be made, either to persuade them to take a firmer attitude or, eventually, to transfer a few of them to London, where they could form a government in exile. Had this last possibility materialized, De Gaulle would perhaps have been put in charge of National Defense in a Cabinet led by Mandel. Thus, on the 18th, while still awaiting the results of the trip, De Gaulle could speak only as a military leader.

During the night of the 17th, a seaplane with a seating capacity of more than forty left London for Biscarrosse, near Bordeaux. The four travelers had ample room; should some of the ministers accept their offer to flee to London, there would be slightly less room on the return flight. Simultaneously, the British government was sending its own seaplane to Bordeaux. Its passengers, the First Lord of the Admiralty, Lord Alexander, and the Colonial Minister, Lord Lloyd, were to gather information on what was happening in French government circles.

At Bordeaux, the four French delegates were confronted with an extremely confused situation. They saw that Marshal Pétain's newly formed government had only one goal: to cease hostilities, though re-establishing order and putting an end to human suffering were also spoken of. One of Monick's friends, who was connected with the new government, dispelled all illusions. "You can be sure that if Marshal Pétain has decided to make the gesture of asking for the terms for an armistice, those terms will be accepted."

Two possibilities were left which might prevent France from giving up the struggle: the first by way of London, the second by way of Algeria. The first consisted of taking a few ministers and Members of Parliament to the English capital, where they could represent the French government. When this was suggested Herriot, the President of the Chamber of Deputies, and Jeanneney, the President of the Senate, answered that it was their duty to remain with the President of the Republic. Therefore that plan was discarded. The second plan, advocated by Mandel, consisted of transporting a few Members of Parliament and some ministers to North Africa, including the President of the Republic. On June 18, the day that the delegates from London were in Bordeaux, there was an official announcement that some members of the government, or VIPs would sail for Casablanca aboard the steamship *Massilia* on the following day. If that was so, Monick and Pleven and Monnet could only encourage French politicians to leave for Morocco; they themselves returned to London on the seaplane, as lightly loaded as before. They had lost most of their illusions about the likelihood of avoiding an armistice. All in all, their mission had been a failure. Indeed, news came on the next day that Germany had agreed to open negotiations for an armistice. It was then that the unofficial warning to Monick took on its full significance. There was every chance that the armistice would be signed. France would lay down its arms, thus breaking its agreements with England.

From that moment De Gaulle ceased to be a military leader trying to reorganize new forces and to continue the struggle. By disowning the Bordeaux government, he took political responsibility on himself. De Gaulle had become a rebel as far as Pétain was concerned. The French Embassy in London received three messages in succession from Bordeaux, each requesting that the ex-Under Secretary of State return to his post in France.

The first message came on June 18. The Minister of War informed De Gaulle by telegraph, through the medium of the French military attaché in London, that he was being returned to active duty and was to come back to France without delay. The following day, June 19, another telegram arrived in which the Minister of War asked the French military attaché to let him know immediately if the order requesting De Gaulle's return to France had reached the General. If not, the order was to be repeated. On June 20, the French military attaché informed the Minister of War by telegram that the order dated June 19, 1940, had reached General de Gaulle, and that this order had been repeated.

On June 22, the Minister of War temporarily removed General de Gaulle's rank. A decree which would retire him from the army in the interests of discipline had been submitted to the President of the Republic for his signature. On June 23, by decree of the President of the Republic, De

Gaulle was put on the retired list—an opportunity which he declined.

And so the break was complete. On the London radio, De Gaulle's attitude toward Marshal Pétain's government became increasingly hostile. On June 26, speaking over the microphone to Marshal Pétain in person, he attacked him so savagely that he sometimes distorted the truth. He quoted as one of the conditions of the armistice accepted by the French government: "Our navy, our planes, our tanks, our arms, to be delivered intact, so that the enemy can use them against our own allies." In reality, the sinking of the French fleet in November, 1942, was to prove conclusively that there had been no question of surrendering it to the enemy.

On June 28, 1940, the British Minister of Information, Duff Cooper, and the Chief of the Imperial General Staff, Sir John Dill, failed to contact Mandel in Casablanca. As a result, the English War Cabinet recognized General de Gaulle as "the leader of the Free French." At this point De Gaulle resolved "to take under his authority all Frenchmen residing in British territory or who may arrive there." The decisive words had been spoken. From then on, the authority of the government headed by Marshal Pétain would be opposed by another "authority." That "authority" considered itself the sole legitimate one and it was to succeed, over the next four years, in making the Allied governments and the majority of the French people share in this conviction.

DE GAULLE IS CONDEMNED TO DEATH

On August 2, 1940, at Clermont-Ferrand, before the court-martial in the 13è Région, the bailiff summoned the accused, who, of course, did not answer. The government prosecutor presented a very brief indictment. In it he quoted three or four sentences from De Gaulle's speeches on the B.B.C. The tribunal, after deliberating behind closed doors, gave its verdict on the six different charges brought up by the prosecution.

The first charge was that De Gaulle was guilty of having conspired with England for the purpose of making England declare hostilities against France. The court acquitted him on that charge.

He was found guilty, however, on the five other charges, by five votes to two. De Gaulle was successively convicted of having supported the interests of England against those of France in his radio broadcasts; of having incited French soldiers and sailors to place themselves in the service of England; of having exposed certain Frenchmen to the risk of reprisals by making broadcasts which would persuade the enemy that the clauses of the armistice were not being, or would not be, observed; of having defected abroad in time of war; and of having done so at a time of siege.

A verdict of guilty on these last five charges meant the death penalty, military degradation, confiscation of all property and personal effects, for Charles André Joseph Marie de Gaulle. He was also ordered to pay the costs of the case.

At 11:15 A.M., the session was over. It had been very dull, unenlivened by any debates or incidents. It had lasted hardly one hour. The judges left, glad to have finished early enough to lunch at home. They had the feeling of having finished with a disagreeable, but necessary, formality.

When he saw the judgment, Marshal Pétain is said to have written with his own hand the words, "Will not be executed."

De Gaulle 1941-1964 – Vicissitudes

and Paradoxes of a Statesman

JULY 14, 1940, IN LONDON

The French national holiday was celebrated in mourning, less than a month after General de Gaulle's installation in London and his appeal over the B.B.C. It was the first July 14 after the defeat and the occupation of French soil by the German army. How different from the one that had been celebrated the previous year, when the entire population had cheered the army everyone still believed invincible as it paraded through Paris. That day had been the one hundred and fiftieth anniversary of the taking of the Bastille. Everyone then believed the Republic would last forever. But on July 14, 1940, the German troops were in Paris, and the Republic had in fact been abolished four days previously, by a vote of the National Assembly which gave Marshal Pétain full powers to set up a new regime, the *État Français*.

At Vichy, in front of the Monument to the War Dead, a few hundred soldiers, their faces still hardened by war and defeat, evoked the 100,000 recent deaths and the two million prisoners. The Marshal reviewed them, wearing the uniform he had worn at Verdun. Elsewhere, in the different capitals of the world, there were varied reactions to the French national holiday; during an open-air concert in Washington, the

"Marseillaise" was struck up, messages of sympathy were sent to the French colony in Ottawa, in Berlin there was self-congratulation and jeering in Madrid.

In London, a few hundred soldiers who had escaped from Dunkirk or Narvik were cheered by the crowd as they paraded past the Cenotaph dedicated, not to the French war dead, but to the English. They were reviewed by the most recent appointment among French generals, General de Gaulle, who had in fact just been transferred to the retired list for disobeying the order sent him to return to France.

This handful of men, under the orders of a leader whose position was irregular, seemed of no importance in contrast to all the governments or all the armies around them, compared, for instance, to the British government and the British army, which were preparing to resist on their so far untouched soil. It did not even represent anything compared to the Belgians, the Dutch, and the Luxembourgers who were, at least, represented in London by legitimate governments in exile. Nor did it carry any weight when compared to the government in Vichy, where the French National Assembly had granted Marshal Pétain and President Pierre Laval the constitutional power to govern and administer France. It represented less than nothing compared to the United States and the U.S.S.R., which had not yet intervened in the war; both of these giants seemed destined to bring their immense resources to bear— America on the side of England; Russia on the side of Germany because of the terms of the German-Soviet Pact. It stood for even less by comparison to Hitlerian Germany, whose victorious armies had conquered and occupied five countries in ten months: Poland, Holland, Luxembourg, Belgium, and France.

And yet, four years later, in August, 1944, the lonely and rebellious General of London was to return to Paris as head of a French government recognized by the Allies. It was he who would have Marshal Pétain and his ministers put on trial.

Two years later still, in 1946, he was to resign voluntarily, believing that the French party game, inherited from the Third Republic, prevented him from properly governing the country. Then, for twelve years, he was to stay aloof from power, influencing French politics, which he despised, by the threat of his return and by his attempts, though fruitless, to establish another *Rassemblement*, similar to the war-time grouping, among his compatriots. During this period he composed his *Memoirs*, in which he related, and sometimes amended in his own way, the events in which he had been involved.

Then came May, 1958. His country was undergoing a period of great crisis. The continuation of the Algerian War threatened not only the unity of France but also spread the fear that military leaders, backed by the European inhabitants of North Africa, would attempt a *Putsch* against the legal government.

And suddenly, De Gaulle was on the scene again, returned to power, altering the Constitution and temporarily soothing the temper of France by promising to keep the French flag flying over Algiers. This did not prevent him from signing a peace with the rebels at Évian in 1962, a peace that set the seal on the withdrawal of the French government and on the evacuation of French inhabitants. In spite of the furious reactions aroused by this *volte face*, and in spite of repeated attempts on his life, some of which he barely escaped, De Gaulle remained in power.

After settling the affairs of France, De Gaulle was to become one of the most influential and active world personalities. Wildly admired by some, overcriticized and feared by others, he is recognized as having a power in world affairs that bears no relation to his country's limited material resources.

De Gaulle has gone a long way since July 14, 1940. How was this possible, and what were the stages of his growth? De Gaulle's early political education can give us a clue.

THE GENERAL'S ORIGINS

This savior of France, this restorer of the Republic and future champion of the Free World, was not a Republican by education or background. He became a Republican through his use of reason, through opposition to the dictatorships that threatened the Free World, and through opposition to Pétain, who had abolished parliamentary rule in France.

Family tradition and background insured that in De Gaulle's formative years he would be a monarchist. In his youth, he was a sympathizer with the *Action Française* movement led by Charles Maurras, who wished to see an authoritarian regime re-established in France, a regime of hereditary monarchs intent on protecting Frenchmen, and the independence of the state, from all the political, economic, and financial pressures that characterize the modern world. Freedom was not understood in the democratic sense, with its checks and balances, parliamentary institutions and a multiplicity of political parties. Maurras despised parliamentary systems and tended to advocate a corporative regime, in which the great bodies of the state, the local authorities, and the professional organizations would allow Frenchmen to demonstrate their opinions not with the political ballot, but within the framework of their "real" lives. Indeed, he drew the distinction between the *legal nation* (*pays légal*), made up of the passing political institutions of the Republic which he loathed, and the *real nation* (*pays réel*), made up of all the Frenchmen who continued to work, live, and sometimes die for their country whatever the regime. Maurras was also a nationalist, at home as well as abroad. At home he was hostile to strangers, to "half-breeds" who lived on French soil. He was anti-Semitic after the fashion of the Middle Ages, as deliberately as, but less brutally than, the Nazis; he did not want the Jews exterminated, but he denied them the right to perform certain functions within the nation. Abroad he thought that the doctrine of *France Seule* was capable of insuring the security and the prosperity of the nation, a chauvinistic position still defensible in the nineteenth century, but, at present, incapable of taking into account the inevitable regrouping of nations into great opposing power blocs.

De Gaulle is certainly no longer a disciple of Maurras in the strict sense of the word. But equally certainly, he was profoundly influenced by this movement which has left its traces on him, even though he disowns all its anachronisms and obsolete policies. At any rate, he owes to it his sense of the state as opposed to the mere "regime," his penchant for French greatness, and his disdain for the parliamentary and the party system. But there is emphatically no trace of anti-Semitism in him.

De Gaulle received his formal education at a "free" school, in other words, a Catholic school, in the rue de Vaugirard in Paris, where his father was *Préfet des Études*. "The students at Vaugirard came chiefly from the dignified, strict, and traditional-minded provincial nobility. At that period, the nobility's fortunes were not flourishing, but it did without luxuries in order to preserve its traditions and keep its children at their fathers' school. The younger boys wore the same uniforms with velvet collars that their elder brothers had worn. The honors list read like a collection of country titles. In the same class were found the names of Enguerrand de Marigny, Montalembert d'Essay, de Salignac-Fénelon, de Gibergue, Didry de Baudot, de Clausade, Dunoyer de Segonzac, and de Crécy. . . ."*

Henri de Gaulle, the General's father, ruled this little hierarchical world with the strict discipline which trained

---

* See Roger Wild's excellent article "De Vaugirard au Quartier Latin" (*Revue des Deux Mondes*, 1962). Wild was a schoolmate of Charles de Gaulle and his description is confirmed by others among my correspondents.

Marshal de Lattre de Tassigny, Marshal Leclerc de Haute-clocque, Cardinal Gerlier, and Georges Bernanos, but he was also a man who inspired respect and affection. At first he had intended to serve in a specialized branch of the army, and had been admitted to the Polytechnique just before the war of 1870. After being wounded at the battles of Stains and Le Bourget, he became a teacher. He retained a rather military silhouette, tempered by much kindness. On Saturday mornings, wearing a frock coat, "he used to come into the schoolroom, to read out solemnly the weekly grades"; he would accentuate his pronunciation when the marks were good, but "when they were bad, he did not stress them, for he liked to praise more than to blame."

What sort of relationship was there between him and his most illustrious pupil, who happened to be his own son, Charles? First of all, no favoritism, nothing in the performance of his duties which would set his son apart from the other pupils; a schoolfellow has described how when Henri de Gaulle had his son as one of his pupils in 1901, he pretended not to remember his son's name, either to tease him or to show impartiality. "So-and-so," he would say, "you may . . ."

Nevertheless, that "so-and-so" was a subject of particular interest to him, and of mixed feelings of satisfaction and anxiety. He confided to one of his most intimate friends in a tone of some admiration, "Charles worries me a great deal. He is very intelligent, but he is very adventuresome." The memory of men is often stylized and deformed; it has doubtless transformed this judgment into something more categorical than it was intended to be. There is no doubt, though, that Charles de Gaulle always believed in his mission, even as an adolescent.

Another correspondent gives us further proof of this. After the vote in favor of the secularization of schools, the School of the Immaculate Conception was closed. The Jesuits in charge emigrated to Belgium and started a new school at Antoing, near Tournai and Fontenoy, to which Charles de Gaulle followed them. At the end of one school year, before the student departed for vacation, young Charles is said to have thanked his religious teacher ceremonially, in the name of his class, and to have declared: "The future shall be great, for we shall forge it."

Though the future liberator of France was born into a royalist family, and was early on indoctrinated with authoritarian concepts and respect for the state, he was at the same time influenced by his father's deep sense of justice. During the great crisis which marked the passage of France from the nineteenth to the twentieth century—the Dreyfus Affair— Henri de Gaulle had believed in the innocence of the Jewish officer, placing the cause of truth above the necessity of protecting the army or the state.

Both aspects of Charles de Gaulle's background surely played a role in his later dealings with the Republic.

DE GAULLE IN LONDON:
JUNE 18–OCTOBER 27, 1940: THE WAR LEADER

This, then, was the background of the man who in June, 1940, as a result of an extraordinary succession of events, found himself representing France in the Free World.

To start with, his only aim was to rally round him the Frenchmen who wanted to continue the struggle, and those French colonies which did not accept the armistice. In the beginning in London, the problem was not to set up a proper government or to adopt a political attitude; it was enough to regroup his scattered forces and to build up more of them. This in itself was an overwhelming task, especially for a man almost entirely isolated. On August 29, he announced over the London radio that France was still in a state of war: "The crime of the armistice is to have capitulated as though France had no Empire. The crime of the armistice is to have underestimated the immense and intact forces that we were keeping in the Empire. The crime of the armistice is to have disarmed the Empire so that the enemy can dispose of it. . . . I call to duty each French territory for the task of national defense. . . ."

Events soon gave their reply to this appeal; one by one, the French overseas territories drew away from Vichy and went over to De Gaulle. The procession began on July 22, when the French population and administration of the New Hebrides joined the Free French movement. This territory in Oceania, however, consisted of an Anglo-French condominium and it is possible that British influence on the French residents played a direct part in their decision. On July 26, a clearer sign was given when the first African colony, the Ivory Coast, allied itself with the Free French. This example was followed by the important territories that made up French Equatorial Africa. On August 26, Tchad officially seceded through the efforts of its Governor General, Félix Eboué, a Negro, who showed himself to be a great servant of France. On the 27th, it was the turn of the Cameroons, where Captain Leclerc, liberator of Paris four years later and future Marshal of France, daringly established his authority at Douala. On the 28th, after a small *Putsch*, the Resistance in Brazzaville seized power and joined De Gaulle. Those three days were called *les trois glorieuses*, evoking the days of 1830 which saw the end of the absolutist monarchy of Charles X in France.

Other French territories, scattered throughout the world, were to follow these first examples. On August 31, it was Tahiti and the Marquesas Islands; on September 9, the French establishments in India, and on September 24, New Caledonia. Compared to the colonies which remained faithful to Vichy and which respected the armistice, this still did not count for very much. The few hundred volunteers of July 14 in London, however, had now became an army of about thirty thousand men, even though they were scattered over four continents. De Gaulle was no longer the modern version of *Jean sans Terre* that he had been when he arrived in London. He controlled some French territories. He could believe, and the British who had gambled on him could also believe, that the movement would spread and that Gaullism would, inch by inch, colony by colony, nibble away at the entire French Empire, and return considerable forces to the fray, on the side of Great Britain.

Unfortunately, on September 25, an unsuccessful Anglo-Gaullist landing at Dakar, capital of French West Africa, put an end to all these hopes. Contrary to what Winston Churchill and De Gaulle had believed, the armed forces and the warships responsible for Dakar's defense refused to join the Free French. They met the British fleet with cannon fire and forced it to turn back. This was a very serious failure for De Gaulle; English policy immediately drew its own conclusions. In the course of some secret talks with the Vichy government, the English government declared, on September 27, that it was inclined not to back any new attempts by the Gaullists on a territory of the French Empire, on condition that Pétain's government agree not to attack British ships and ports, to recognize British aid to the Free French, and to guarantee that the navy and the colonies still under the control of Vichy would not come under German or Italian influence. These negotiations were interrupted after a meeting between Pétain and Hitler on October 24, at Montoire, where a closer policy of collaboration between France and Germany was announced. This did nothing, however, to alter the fact that De Gaulle had suffered a severe defeat, and he was to have to wait for more than two years before the French colonies of West and North Africa, which had not gone over to him, were delivered by his political adversaries, other Frenchmen grouped around General Giraud. Nor did the actions of Vichy alter the fact that De Gaulle, from then on, could expect the Allies to drop him if they found it to their advantage. During those two years of waiting, De Gaulle neither despaired nor remained inactive. From the war leader he had been in the beginning, he slowly changed himself into the leader of a government.

OCTOBER 27, 1940–SEPTEMBER 23, 1941: BIRTH OF A GOVERNMENT

On October 27, a month after the failed *Putsch* at Dakar, De Gaulle published an ordinance which defined the organization of Free France for the duration of the war and set up "Le Conseil de Défense de l'Empire." It was not yet a government, properly speaking, but a war council which would have to resign or transform itself on the day the war ended. On November 11, at Brazzaville, De Gaulle defined its reason for existence: "Since those who were our leaders have given up their duty, through panic or despair, we have decided, in shame and in grief, to recognize them no longer. . . . We will act so that the Fatherland may have its share in the victory, and it is we who will restore its honor, its greatness, and its happiness. . . ."

On November 16, making use of one of the most popular habits and privileges of a French government, he conceived of a new decoration, and by decree, founded the *Ordre de la Libération* to reward the individuals and the military and civilian groups which had played an outstanding role in the liberation of France and its Empire.

It was not until December 28 that General de Gaulle gave direct instructions for the first time to the Frenchmen who had remained in France under the Occupation, asking them to remain in their homes in the Occupied Zone for an hour on Janurary 1, between three and four o'clock, which corresponded to the hour from two to three o'clock in the Free Zone. This would be a protest against the presence of the enemy, and "by this immense plebiscite of silence, France will let the world know that it sees its future only in freedom, its greatness only in independence, its salvation only in victory." On New Year's Day, at the specified hour, the streets were emptied, the squares and the boulevards were nearly deserted; the call had been heard. France had recognized De Gaulle.

The "Conseil de Défense de l'Empire" did not wait long to take new political decisions. On February 22, it issued a declaration concerning the integrity of the Empire and France's rights in the world. "France's temporary disaster can in no way justify any attempt whatsoever made by foreign powers either on the integrity of its Empire or on the rights of France in any part of the world." This statement was outwardly aimed at the possessions Vichy might agree to give up, specifically Indochina. But it could also be interpreted as a warning against any territorial ambitions on the part of the Allies.

On June 8, De Gaulle gave the most dazzling and unchallengeable proof of his strength, by ordering his troops in the Near East to "take up again the struggle for the liberation of France." This euphemism disguised a very terrible truth. It not only meant that the Free French forces would enter the war under the command of General Catroux, who had been chosen by De Gaulle as commander in chief in the Levant and delegate general and plenipotentiary of the leader of the Free French for the states of the Levant. It also meant that a fratricidal war was about to be fought; in its course, Gaullist troops, side by side with the British, would be obliged to fight against French troops loyal to Vichy. Perhaps this terrible tragedy was necessary so that France would still be in the Levant when Vichy was ousted.

On September 23, 1941, the "Conseil de Défense de l'Empire" gave way to a "Conseil National Français," which was the authentic embryo of a provisional government. In principle, this "Conseil" would be in power until France was in a position to freely select its representatives. Three of its members were military men: the President, General de Gaulle; the War Commissioner, General Legentilhomme; and the Naval and Air Commissioner, Admiral Muselier. Three of its members were civilians: the Foreign Affairs Commissioner, Dejean; the Commissioner of Justice and of National Education, Professor René Cassin; and the Commissioner of Economic Affairs, Hervé Alphand, later French Ambassador to the United States.

These "Commissioners" were appointed by decree, without any of the usual democratic processes. Not one of them had been chosen from among the few Members of Parliament who had come over to London. It is true that, at the time, Members of Parliament were still being rather badly received at the headquarters of Free France. A deputy from the Aisne, Pierre Bloch, later testified to this in his memoirs: De Gaulle even intervened personally to make it clear to one of the Deputies, Félix Gouin, that neither Gouin nor his colleagues had any right to represent French public opinion.

All of De Gaulle's decisions and all these steps taken to consolidate his power were, of course, less concerned with the usual processes of democratic regimes than with the demands of an exceptional situation. His task was to insure the destiny of France. In London and Washington, the question began to be asked: was De Gaulle a genuine believer in democracy or not? Some French émigrés, who had grouped themselves into rival factions, helped circulate the rumor that De Gaulle stood for personal power and against democracy.

Actually, De Gaulle never ignored the fact that his historic mission was to restore democracy to France. He never stopped proclaiming that the Republican regime had been illegally abolished by the Vichy government, and that the Republic continued though Pétain *seemed* to be in power. But, for all that, he did not want to fall back into the old parliamentary system, the party system, which had led France into crisis and defeat. He had his own concept of the Republic and his own concept of freedom. These concepts might surprise experienced parliamentarians, whether British or French; they surprised his American allies even more.

This personal concept revealed itself for the first time in an extraordinary episode that took place in December, 1941, when De Gaulle occupied the islands of Saint Pierre and Miquelon. At this time he revealed two aspects of his policy: his casualness and almost insulting intransigence toward his allies; and his use of the Republican regime.

DE GAULLE'S FIRST REFERENDUM: SAINT PIERRE AND MIQUELON (CHRISTMAS, 1941)

On Christmas Day of 1941, the inhabitants of the little archipelago of Saint Pierre and Miquelon, near Newfoundland, were asked to hold a referendum. On the previous day, to their surprise, they had seen a flotilla of Free French naval forces approach their shores. A detachment of marines had landed on their soil and taken over their little territory without a shot. In spite of the restricted scope of the operation, it was nonetheless an important affair. First of all, De Gaulle had decided to take over the islands, which had until then remained under the authority of the Vichy government, against the express wish of the Americans. This was the first of his challenges to the United States. It was also the first time since June 18, 1940, that De Gaulle was asking a people of French descent, not under colonial jurisdiction, to join him.

The problem was not merely to land and to occupy the islands, but to be accepted by referendum, unanimously if possible. In this way, De Gaulle would appear to have been recognized by the first population of French descent which he had encountered, and thus symbolize the reception he would be given by metropolitan France when victory finally came. It would be his investiture in the eyes of his angry and halting allies.

According to Admiral Muselier's statistics, the 4,000 inhabitants of the island included a strong majority of Gaullists (70 per cent), a sizeable minority of undecided people or pro-Vichyites (at least 20 per cent), and a very small number of pro-Nazi collaborators. If the question asked at the referendum had been straightforward ("Are you for De Gaulle or for Pétain?") then a 20 per cent minority hostile to the new arrivals would have to be accepted. Such a percentage was much too much for De Gaulle's prestige vis-à-vis his allies, Vichy—and himself.

And so, inaugurating a practice in which he was to become past master, De Gaulle had the plebiscite worded in terms that made it almost impossible for anyone not to vote for him. Instead of the painful alternatives of Pétain or De Gaulle, he imposed another: "Are you for De Gaulle or for the Axis powers? You will have to choose between the cause of Free France and that of collaboration with the powers which starve, humiliate, and martyr our country." The ballot sheets had two questions on them: one of the questions had to be crossed out by the electors, the other would represent their choice "Joining Free France—Collaboration with the Axis Powers." How could anyone cross out the first and keep the second? How could anyone admit that he was for Hitler or Mussolini? Thus

651 votes for Free France
11 votes for collaboration

As for the 20 per cent who would normally have voted against De Gaulle, they added up to a slightly smaller percentage of abstentions or blank ballots, totaling 140 votes.

And so, as in all cleverly prepared referendums of this sort, there was a majority of 98 per cent for him among votes cast.

This is how De Gaulle uses the electorate, the fountainhead of all Republican power. He conditions the voters with the questions he asks them and with the propaganda which surrounds those questions.

Were De Gaulle, God forbid, to want to end the Republican regime, he would probably prepare a referendum giving no genuine alternative such as "Are you for the suppression of the Republic or for doubling the income tax?" And the Republic would be repealed—in the most Republican fashion possible.

De Gaulle's aim, however, is to restore the Republic, to adapt it both to his personal concepts and at the same time to the needs of our age, or at least to its needs as he sees them.

DE GAULLE AND THE REPUBLIC: ALGIERS (NOVEMBER, 1943– AUGUST, 1944)

De Gaulle's restoration of the Republic began in Algiers, in November, 1943.

A year earlier, on November 8, 1942, a small handful of members of the French Resistance had set up a gigantic plot in Algeria, Tunisia, and Morocco to facilitate the landing of American troops as well as provoke the re-entry of the French forces in Africa into the war.

De Gaulle was in London at the time, and the entire operation was prepared without his knowledge, took place without his being warned. Another French general, Giraud, had been given command of it: Giraud, whose sensational escapes from German prisons had won him tremendous prestige.

Backed by clandestine French forces, which neutralized the pro-Pétain authorities of Algiers, the landing succeeded in Algeria and in Morocco, but German troops got to Tunisia before the Americans, and thereby occupied this French protectorate for seven months before finally being expelled with the help of French divisions in Africa.

At first the man put in charge of French North Africa was Admiral Darlan, an ex-Prime Minister of Marshal Pétain who was accidentally in Algiers on D-day because he had come to be near his son, who was gravely ill. Darlan was assassinated on December 25, 1942.

Giraud, who replaced him, had only one ambition: to help win the war. His motto was "Only one aim, victory." But to attain this end, he accepted aid from every quarter, ex-Vichyites along with members of the Resistance, as long as they were all determined to fight the Germans. In the beginning, he even represented himself as Marshal Pétain's delegate and heir. In view of France's actual situation, he believed it premature to make political decisions. Everyone should concentrate on the business of war, and postpone until victory any consultation with the liberated French about what regime would then be chosen.

De Gaulle's policy was exactly the opposite. From London, he asserted that there had to be a break with the Vichy government, and that all who had belonged to, or even served, Vichy had to be eliminated. He also declared that the Republic had been illegally abolished and that it had to be restored by annulling all the legislation which had been put through by Vichy after the defeat.

For six months the France that was at war, the Resistance against the Germans, had two governments: that of De Gaulle in London and that of Giraud in Algiers. This situation could not continue for long. There were extended and painful negotiations, in which, little by little, Giraud gave up his own position and drew closer to that of his rival. After De Gaulle's arrival in Algiers on May 30, 1943, a new government body was created, the Comité Français de Libération Nationale, presided over by both leaders, and though in principle the two men were supposed to be on an equal footing, from the very start it was De Gaulle's influence that prevailed. In a short time his political concepts triumphed, and Giraud was finally eased out in November, 1943.

De Gaulle's victory led to two types of measures. The first

involved his total rupture with Vichy: De Gaulle resolved to dismiss all ex-members of Marshal Pétain's government and to bring to trial those among them who had actively collaborated with the Germans. Secondly, De Gaulle decided to reinstall the Republic.

DE GAULLE SETS THE PURGES UNDER WAY

Ever since his first days in North Africa De Gaulle had shown determination to break away from Vichy. Without taking Giraud into consideration, he demanded and obtained the removal of an ex-Vichy minister, Peyrouton, who was then Governor General of Algiers, and replaced him with General Catroux, a Gaullist from the very beginning.

Soon after the elimination of Giraud, De Gaulle went even further with the purge of Pierre Pucheu in March, 1944. Pucheu had been Minister of the Interior in the Vichy government, and was charged with responsibility for executing hostages and taking arbitrary action in co-operation with the Nazis in occupied France. Though he had gone over to the side of the Free French, he had been arrested in Algiers and was tried by a "military tribunal with special powers," which condemned him to death. In the atmosphere of the times and under the pressure of the forces of the Resistance, especially of the Communists, it could not have been otherwise.

Pucheu's only chance of avoiding execution was an appeal for pardon that his defense lawyers, Maître Buttin and Maître Trappe, addressed to De Gaulle, who, as chief of government, was acting as Head of State. The matter became a grave question of conscience for De Gaulle. A man's life was at stake, and in his innermost heart, the General thought Pucheu, if not innocent, at least forgivable. But the man was the first Vichy minister to stand trial, and what De Gaulle decided about Pucheu would indicate whether later trials would be oriented toward politics—"reasons of state"—or toward justice and charity—the humane side of law. The precedent created here would weigh on the future of France and on events after the Liberation.

Henri Frenay, one of the members of De Gaulle's Cabinet, confided in Maître Buttin that General de Gaulle had told him that he hadn't been able to sleep for two days, not knowing what decision to make. But once the decision had been made, it became irrevocable. When Maîtres Buttin and Trappe came to ask for Pucheu's pardon, De Gaulle told them: "I concede that it is a political matter. Like you, I shall not go over the proceedings again, which are of slight importance. There is almost nothing in the dossier itself. I regret the fact that some of the evidence took on the character of set speeches that were out of place. We are living through an awful tragedy, which has its origins in the fact that some people believed it was their duty to lay down arms before every other means had been exhausted. This led us to that terrible policy of collaboration and all its present consequences. I do not doubt that some collaborated in good faith, and I am convinced that Pucheu belongs to that number. I am even sure that he was one of those who, within the framework of that terrible policy, did their best to counter the Germans and to surrender as little as possible. . . .

"I am aware of the deep agitation the trial has provoked in the minds of the public. Good Frenchmen, in good faith, want his death, especially the ones in France who are suffering. All are under the sway of their passions. I must rise above my passions and only reasons of state must dictate my judgment. . . .

"I continue to esteem Monsieur Pucheu. Let him know that I am positive his intentions were good and that he was sincere. In this tragedy we are going through, that France is going through, when everyone is suffering, we individuals do not count. Our only guide must be the good of the state. . . .

"I would like you to add this too. Be sure you tell Monsieur

Pucheu that, if I go to France one day, I give him my formal word of honor, I take this oath in your presence: I have children, so does he. I will personally, I insist, personally, do all I humanly can to provide for the moral and physical education of his children. I will do everything to avoid their having to suffer too much for the decision I may be called to make."

As far as repression and purges are concerned, De Gaulle's external manner and his constant use of the argument for reasons of state conceal scruples of justice and humanity. Yet this does not alter the fact that in the end Pucheu was executed.

It is reasons of state that always account for his legal trials of opponents—in 1944, against the members of the Vichy government, and in 1962, against the Algerian generals who rebelled against him. Reasons of state determined by political motives often conflict with justice and charity. De Gaulle knows this and it pains him, for it goes against the grain of both his Christian upbringing and his French humanist education. But he goes ahead, faithful to the motto that the salvation of the fatherland is the supreme law.

De Gaulle restores the Republic

At the same time that he began the purges, De Gaulle restored the Republic. To do this, he had to rely on an assembly that would act as a parliament. Gathering together the members of the Senate and of the Chamber of Deputies was out of the question. Most of them had remained in Occupied France and had voted for the abolition of the Republican regime on July 10, 1940. Nor was it possible to hold new elections while France remained under Nazi domination. Also, De Gaulle did not precisely relish the idea of having his power curtailed by members of a parliament. The problem was how, given the circumstances and the General's policy, to create an *ersatz* parliament which would give him the apparent support of public opinion in the eyes of the Allies and the French people.

The solution which, except for a few minor changes, he on February 25, 1943, by the Comité National Français de applied later in Algiers, appeared in a memorandum published Londres (in other words, by himself). De Gaulle and Giraud had not yet met. De Gaulle had not gone to North Africa, but the negotiations with Giraud had already begun, and De Gaulle, confronted by a rival who still showed some attachment to the Vichy government, had to set himself up as the champion of the Republic.

In his memorandum he anticipated the calling of a "Consultative Assembly," whose rights were far more limited than those of an ordinary parliament.

As its name indicated, this Assembly was to have neither the power to overthrow the government nor to make laws: its role was to be limited to public discussion of the decisions made by the government. Also, and this is the most important point, this nucleus of a parliament was to be constituted very differently from an ordinary assembly. Its members would be appointed by the government, instead of being elected. It would, of course, include some of the Deputies and Senators of the former Parliament who had not approved the signing of the armistice or collaborated with the enemy and would exclude all those who had joined Vichy. But these ex-Members of Parliament would make up only a minor part of the Assembly. The remainder, the majority, would be chosen from among representatives of the Resistance organizations, the elected bodies of the liberated territories of the Empire, economic groups, trade unions, the academics in the Empire, and the French Citizens' Associations abroad.

De Gaulle would therefore have a minority of the representatives of the nation chosen from the ranks of the political parties, and a majority from apolitical groups which stood for the genuine fighting life of the nation. It was a profound innovation in the workings of Republican institutions. For De Gaulle, it was a concept of democracy to which he would always remain faithful in principle, but which he would never actually achieve in practice.

As will be seen later, the Consultative Assembly which met in Algiers on November 3, 1943, corresponded to De Gaulle's declaration. For a brief time, De Gaulle could believe that he was setting up a Republic on the pattern that he desired. But very soon after the Liberation and the return of the Consultative Assembly to France, the influence of the Resistance movements diminished, while that of the former political parties reasserted itself and grew steadily stronger.

With the rebirth of prewar parliamentary intrigue, De Gaulle resigned on January 20, 1946. By leaving power in this fashion, De Gaulle left French politics in a troubled and uncertain condition. The Constituent Assembly, elected in October, 1945, to give a new Constitution to the nation, had not yet achieved its goal and would not achieve it in one attempt. The country rejected a first Constitution in a referendum on May 5, 1946. It barely accepted a second one, endorsed by only a third of the electorate, on October 13 of that same year (9,263,416 voting for—8,143,986 voting against—with 8,467,537 abstentions).

This Constitution gave full powers to the parties which governed through the National Assembly. There was no other strong governmental body to oppose them. The government was responsible to the Assembly and could be overturned by it, and even the election of a chief of state was reserved to Parliament. De Gaulle had thus definitively failed in his attempts to renew the Republican regime by flooding it with new forces.

There was nothing for him to do but declare publicly what he thought of the Fourth Republic, which he did in his speech at Bayeux on June 16, 1946. He then tried to group together those Frenchmen who opposed the party system, but after a brilliant start, this attempt also failed. He retired to Colombey-les-Deux-Églises to write his *Memoirs* and wait to be recalled.

DE GAULLE WRITES HIS MEMOIRS

General de Gaulle's *Memoirs* consist of three large volumes. The first two appeared during the period of his retirement, in 1954 and 1956, the third in 1959, a short time after his return to power. It is an impressive work, not only because of its literary merit, but also because of the insights it gives, sometimes without the author's knowledge, into his political concepts and his notions of historical truth.

De Gaulle is a man of letters, one of the greatest French writers of our time: his *Memoirs*, written during the fortunate intervals when politics left him in peace, are an authentic epic. They tell the almost unbelievable tale of an unknown officer's adventure when, in June, 1940, he started to speak in the name of France on a foreign network—of how his amazing prediction was confirmed four years later by the French people, a majority of whom had never heard of him. This story has some of the aspects of a legend, mixing historical fact with poetic license. De Gaulle, a poet of action who makes his own legends come true, wrote the legend of his life in his *Memoirs*. His case is unprecedented in our history. It is as if the *Song of Roland* were written in Roland's own words.

The greater the statesman, and the more important his role in the history of his own country, the more cautiously his memoirs should be treated. Churchill wrote his *Memoirs* to vindicate his actions, as well as those of his countrymen. He sometimes presents events in a light which exaggerates the martial spirit and the political steadfastness of England. The same holds true for De Gaulle, but with the difference that his own personal vindication is more closely interwoven with that of France. For he identified himself with France, and any retouching of his own history also retouched that of France.

The following story provides a curious example of how De Gaulle the historian touched up the history of De Gaulle the statesman.

Before noon on the Sunday after the liberation of Paris, August 27, General Eisenhower, Supreme Commander of the Allied Forces, went to visit General de Gaulle, installed in the War Ministry on the rue Saint-Dominique. De Gaulle was "already surrounded by the traditional Republican guards in their resplendent uniforms." In his memoirs Eisenhower gave a detailed description of the conversation that ensued:

General de Gaulle communicated to me some of his anxieties and problems . . . A serious problem in view of the disorganized state of the city was the speedy establishment of his own authority and the preservation of order. He asked for the temporary loan of two American divisions to use, as he said, as a show of force and to establish his position firmly. My memory flashed back almost two years, to Africa and our political problems of that time. There we had accepted the governmental organization already in existence and never during our entire stay had one of the French officials asked for Allied troops in order to establish or affirm his position as a local administrative authority. Here there seemed a touch of the sardonic in the picture of France's symbol of liberation having to ask for Allied forces to establish and maintain a similar position in the heart of the freed capital.

Nevertheless, I understood De Gaulle's problem, and while I had no spare units to station temporarily in Paris, I did promise him that two of our divisions, marching to the front, would do so through the main avenues of the city. I suggested that while these divisions were passing through Paris they could proceed in ceremonial formation and invited him to review them. I felt that this show of force and De Gaulle's presence on the reviewing stand would accomplish all that he sought. I declined personally to be present at this formation but told him that General Bradley would come back to the city and stand with him on the reviewing platform to symbolize Allied unity.

Because this ceremonial march coincided exactly with the local battle plan it became possibly the only instance in history of troops marching in parade through the capital of a great country to participate in pitched battle on the same day.*

And so, to impress the disorderly elements in Paris, which might escape his control, De Gaulle called for the help of two Allied divisions. It was doubtless painful for him to make this request, and he had to suffer the added vexation of having it turned down. The best that the great American leader could offer was a sham performance to impress the people of Paris.

Contemporary sources, including a film, confirm that the parade took place. De Gaulle did in fact accept Eisenhower's proposal even if it was both inadequate and humiliating.

He accepted it, but with distaste. And so, in his *Memoirs*, he does not even mention it. He gives a very brief and simplified account of his interview with Eisenhower, without touching on the subject of the two American divisions, and simply writes of the one and only French division, the Second Armored Division of Leclerc, then in operation.

But the *Memoirs*, whose facts sometimes raise doubts as to their authenticity, are absolutely trustworthy insofar as they reveal the behavior and the feelings of the author himself.

In the second volume there appears an extraordinarily revealing sentence on De Gaulle's concept of political action. It is not, from the literary standpoint, one of the finest sentences in the book. Others are as finely cut as medallions and delight the reader more; but this one is infinitely more telling than any other:

"In human endeavors, due to a long and slow effort, a sudden, unique spurt may be achieved in different and disparate spheres."

This can only mean that, for De Gaulle, there are two periods of action. There is a first period, which is the time of waiting, of preparation, of almost unnoticed effort, during which events mature imperceptibly. And there is a second

* *Crusade in Europe* (New York: Doubleday, 1948).

period, which is the time of realization, of explosion, of spectacular gestures and resounding decisions, when the development is completed. Then current events go down the Royal Way toward History, and the statesman rushes forward to unravel situations and to resolve problems.

The first is the vulgar period, when the decision is being prepared, and when the leader's will awaits the occasion with the patience of an elephant or the furtiveness of a beast after its prey. And the second is the noble period, when destiny is fulfilled, when the man puts his stamp on the course of events, when he leaves his mark forever, when he sculpts and directs his times. The De Gaulle of the vulgar period is not the De Gaulle of the noble period. The De Gaulle of the waiting period is not the De Gaulle of the period of accomplishments.

During the vulgar period he does not care what he says; his words are merely anecdotal, destined only for current usage. This was evident in his handling of Algeria. Before the time seemed ripe, perhaps before he himself knew what his decision would be, he would say anything at all. He allowed the French in Algiers to believe that he would protect them and that he understood them. While inspecting the various officers' messes in Algiers, the famous *tournée des popotes*, he persuaded the French officers that he wanted them to persevere and to win. He deceived everybody, trapping people in intolerable and insoluble dilemmas from which some tried to escape by rebelling against him, while others ate their words and followed him. Then came the "unique spurt in different and disparate spheres," the triggering of events which put an end to the vulgar period and heralded the period of nobility, if, that is, there is any nobility in reversing one's judgment and in misusing others. Still, when all is said and done, the future seems to have justified the end he sought, if not the means he employed.

The same sequence can be observed in his actions vis-à-vis

the United States. The triggering took place after De Gaulle attended Kennedy's funeral. The President's assassination may have acted as a warning of fate, or perhaps during that brief stay in Washington he measured Kennedy's successor and it seemed to him that, at least in the field of international politics, Johnson was less of an innovator than Kennedy. Whatever the reason, from that moment a chain of events occurred in quick succession, or rather, was provoked by De Gaulle. First came the recognition of China, then the affability toward Cuba, then the increased, or rediscovered, intimacy with South America and with Far Eastern countries—so many unequivocal gestures, unmistakable assertions after a long period of evasion, seeming hesitation, diplomatic cautiousness which killed time in politics and postponed the hour of choice, decision, and action.

Being a scholar and statesman, an eminent man of letters and a distinguished leader, does not make De Gaulle any easier to deal with or to understand. A distinction must always be drawn between the words destined for inclusion in the annals of history, or in his *Memoirs,* and the words intended merely to influence current events.

De Gaulle is a man who listens to himself when he writes but who does not always hear himself speak.

DE GAULLE COMES BACK TO POWER (MAY, 1958)

In his *Memoirs,* De Gaulle showed that he does not have a taste for historical truth or objectivity: his attitudes and opinions vary according to the circumstances so that they can surprise and disappoint those around him. He is so sure of his basic consistency and of his infallibility that the variants he uses to reach his goal do not matter to him; he is almost surprised that they should matter to others.

Secondly, he showed that he is in no hurry; he always counts on time, on the passage of time. It is his great ally. He recalls it in the faraway ages of French history; he accepts it in the present as it unfolds; he senses it in the future, as it will occur. De Gaulle is like an automobile driver, looking at the horizon without caring about the bumps and curves in the road. He risks an accident at each bump in the road, yet he is clever enough and confident enough always to arrive in the end at the goal he has chosen.

These two characteristics, revealed in his *Memoirs*, were strikingly demonstrated in May, 1958, when he returned to power. The army and the Algerian population had called upon De Gaulle to save Algeria from the threat of the F.L.N. rebellion. France was living through one of the worst tragedies in its history. Algeria had been French since 1830 and since then it had been considered part of the French Republic. It was divided into three Departments which, like those in France, were administered by Prefects. It had a population of one million Frenchmen and seven million Arabs; losing Algeria would be for France like losing two great cities, let us say Lyons and Marseilles. Also, the economic and political power of the country was vested, for the most part, in Frenchmen who, in three or four generations, had created the wealth and the prosperity of the three Departments by their labor and competence. Algiers, capital of Algeria, was a great French city where urbanism had been most successful.

On November 1, 1954, the rebellion began. At first it was confined to a few mountainous regions, but it soon spread over a large area, and for the next four years, France had to devote an ever growing military effort to put down the rebellion. In 1956 the Socialist government of Guy Mollet decided to call up some reservists and to prolong the term of conscription so that a larger regular army could add to the resources at the disposal of the High Command.

The French army showed its superiority in every respect wherever it confronted the rebel troops in regular combat. The High Command adapted itself well to the tactics of a guerrilla war, by using the methods of the *maquis*. Many times the "last hour" seemed about to strike. But each time the rebellion would pick up again, for it was supported by international opinion, and it had inaccessible rear bases and inexhaustible reserves both in Tunisia and Morocco. The question of peace was continually postponed, as it is in Vietnam today.

In France, no government was able to end the conflict; they were therefore overthrown, one after the other and with ever greater speed. On May 13, 1958, hysteria reached its peak. The French-Algerian population had begun to rebel against the leaders of the Fourth Republic, and the army seemed ready to intervene and to attempt a *Putsch* against Parliament and the government of Pierre Pflimlin.

On May 28, 1958, the President of the Republic, René Coty, urged De Gaulle to become head of the government. De Gaulle gave his terms, which were twofold: firstly, "he would be given, for a stated time, full powers to act in the present very grave situation," and secondly, "he would be given a mandate, according to a provision stated in the present Constitution, to prepare and to present to the nation by means of a referendum the changes that had to be made in the said Constitution. . . ."

On June 2, he presented himself before the Assembly and got what he demanded: in the beginning he would govern without parliamentary control; later he would be able to change the Constitution.

All this was given him so that he could keep Algeria French. Later, the question would be raised as to whether that was indeed De Gaulle's true intention, or whether it was a pretext that allowed him to return to power and reform the regime.

At first he lavished reassuring statements on the army and the French population of Algeria. The following are a few of his declarations.

To the military leaders: "Never, in my lifetime, will the F.L.N. flag fly over Algiers."

On June 4, hardly three days after his investiture, he was more explicit: "In Algeria, there are only full-fledged French citizens."

In Mostaganem, on June 5, 1958, he ended his speech with the words, "Long live French Algeria!"

At the end of this first trip to Algeria he addressed an Order of the Day to the land, air, and sea forces of Algeria which they must have found comforting:

"During the three splendid days I spent in Algeria, I saw you in action. I know the work which you are doing, under your leaders' orders, with exemplary courage and discipline, to keep Algeria for France and to keep it French. The trust which the population puts in the army, and of which I have had so much proof, convinces me that your efforts in the nation's service will be rewarded by a great national success. France will achieve its aim here: peace, unity, and fraternity."

Three months later, on September 28, 1958, the referendum which would decide Algeria's future was in preparation. At the time, De Gaulle defined what the vote would mean in a seemingly unequivocal fashion:

"In the present circumstances, to answer 'yes' will mean at the very least that the voter wants to act as a full-fledged Frenchman and believes that Algeria must evolve within a French framework."

On October 3, 1958, in Constantine, he may have started to qualify his ideas: "Algeria's future will have a dual basis: its own character, and its close ties with France." But there was nothing yet that prophesied his future endorsement of Algeria for the Algerians. All those who had made his return possible—the population of Algiers which had cheered his name, the generals like Salan who had used it to re-establish trust and order during rioting, and the Committee of Public Safety—had grounds to feel certain that the man of June 18, 1940, now also the man of May, 1958, would again take up his historic mission: once again, he would act against a policy of defeat and guarantee the sovereignty of French territory.

Even the Delegate General in Algeria, on returning from Paris in October, 1958, assured General Challe: "I have just seen the Prime Minister and you can say that the French army will continue the fight to keep Algeria as French soil."

In view of this, the generals did their job. They began by expanding military operations. In March, 1960, these operations had extended so far that the Fourth Vilaya, that of Algiers, and the Mitidja, asked for negotiations and sent three delegates to the Élysée to speak with De Gaulle. Next, the generals were able to take the native population in hand again, multiplying their assurances that France had given her word and that it could be trusted.

But the army leaders were already one step behind. Without saying a word, De Gaulle was considering another solution to the Algerian dilemma. This solution was self-determination, "Algeria for the Algerians," in other words, independence.

At the Élysée, De Gaulle received the three negotiators for a peace that would keep the French in Algiers. At the same time he was secretly negotiating with the G.P.R.A. (Provisional Government of the Algerian Republic), the rebel headquarters, to prepare for Algerian independence. The result of this was that one of the negotiators of the Fourth Vilaya was killed in ambush on his return to Algeria. At the same time his adjutant, the military commissioner Mohamed, began a purge that allowed him to execute 460 to 480 members of the Vilaya which had been involved in the peace negotiations.

And so De Gaulle short-circuited and finally sacrificed those who, in agreement with the French army leaders, turned to him to preserve French Algeria. What could the French generals think or do? They had taken the initiative in the negotiations, thinking they were backed by the civilian government. They now found that they had perjured themselves and lost face before those who had trusted them.

A terrible bout of conscience then began for these generals, and it would continue until the end of the Algerian tragedy. When faced with the necessity of honoring his promises to the army and to all those who had brought him to power, or of accepting the necessities of a new policy, De Gaulle soon made his decision: he broke with those who had backed him. "Can you admit that I may be President of the Council of the Committee of Public Safety," he declared, "and at the same time be carried on the shields of the praetorians?"

The unlucky "praetorians" obviously did not expect to be so designated and so disavowed. The only choice they had, then, was either to betray—in the name of discipline—those who had trusted them, or to rebel in an attempt to stand by their commitments.

"We are told," Challe would declare at his trial, "we are told: 'Obedience, Discipline, and Duty.' And we answer, 'Obedience, yes. Discipline, yes. Duty, yes, unto death and including death, but not unto perjury, ten times, a hundred times repeated. Because we are not domestic animals after all, but human beings, and there is no reason of state, there is no law in the world that can make perjury a man's daily bread.' " Which corresponds to a declaration once made by De Gaulle before a group of officers at Blida: "The army has no politics. It is not up to the army to be political. The army's honor, the army's duty, is merely to serve." But in speaking those words in those circumstances, was the De Gaulle of 1960 fulfilling or denying what he had stated on June 18, 1940? That is the whole question.

Whatever the answer, the fact remains that at Évian, in April, 1962, De Gaulle signed a treaty with the leaders of the Algerian rebellion, making final the secession of Algeria from France and Algeria's independence. He also showed himself without mercy toward the generals who had trusted his first declarations that he would keep France in Algeria. Those generals had rebelled when he changed his course of action and went against his previous commitments. Generals Challe,

Salan, and André Zeller—some of the top leaders of the French army—were tried and sentenced to life imprisonment for making a decision prescribed by their sense of duty and their patriotic sentiments. As for those of North Africa who had set up a terrorist movement called the O.A.S. (Organisation de l'Armée Secrète), they were pitilessly fought and relentlessly tracked. Even the French army, which the O.A.S. had never ceased to acclaim, was given orders to shoot them down.

The Paradoxes of De Gaulle

De Gaulle, one begins to see, is not a simple man. The story of his climb to power and the peaks of his activity as a statesman reveal a set of complexities, and often of paradoxes, which I would like to define by trying to explain four particularly sensitive points in his make-up.

First paradox: Because of his upbringing and his personal inclinations, De Gaulle would have been a monarchist more easily than a republican. He has always remained faithful to the Republic, probably because he has a private conception of it which does not resemble anyone else's. He prefers a direct appeal to the nation by means of a referendum to addressing himself to the people's representatives in Parliament.

Second paradox: De Gaulle saved France from the dictatorships of the Nazis and the Stalinists, whose primary principle is the subjection of everything to reasons of state. Yet he himself often resorts to it, whether to "purge" the Vichy partisans or to condemn the generals who rebelled against him for patriotic reasons. In the name of what principle does he call on justice, when he himself acts arbitrarily?

Third paradox: De Gaulle is both a writer and a statesman. He has no more succeeded in reconciling these two parallel vocations than anyone else. A statesman has to consider the facts as they are; a writer imagines them as he would have wished them to be. This paradox cuts very deep, and perhaps it explains some of the General's seeming contradictions.

Fourth paradox: De Gaulle demands absolute obedience on the part of his generals, his ministers, and his admirers. Yet he himself began by disobeying in June, 1940, and he owes to that disobedience his rise to power. In what name can he condemn others for doing what gave him his legitimacy?

EXPLANATION OF THE PARADOXES

These apparent paradoxes contribute to the uniqueness and to the greatness of the man. At the same time they make him difficult to understand, and, to some, unbearable. They are primarily the result of two permanent character traits in De Gaulle which appear throughout his career and which are usually in conflict: his intransigence and his empiricism. Somehow De Gaulle manages to reconcile these two irreconcilable traits, and in this respect he resembles many great revolutionaries, men of doctrine and action. He brings to mind something Lenin once said: you need a maximum of intransigence in doctrine to allow yourself a minimum of flexibility in practice. De Gaulle, however, sometimes gives the impression that his minimum and his maximum vary.

His intransigence first appears in the circumstances that made his rise to power possible. Faced with a threatening, then tragic situation in France, from 1934 to 1944, De Gaulle behaved ruthlessly both to those responsible for that state of affairs and to those who took advantage of it. He was uncompromisingly intransigent in his attitude toward the Vichy government and in his attitude toward the political party system. His most vital instinct took over when he confronted the circumstances that almost led to France's doom. It was a reaction in keeping with the need for national salvation, and he could not have acted otherwise.

But a study of his tactics reveals his empiricism. Whether

or not he knows his end from the very start, he obviously wavers in his course. At each step he seems to hesitate, to change tack, to alter his position and to take up a new attitude which allows him to keep his position momentarily or to advance, even if he has to go back on his word later. And, most important, he always keeps his real goal hidden until he has achieved it. This makes his relations with his allies particularly difficult to understand.

Capping the two, linking his intransigence to his empiricism, is the question of De Gaulle's ideology—does he have a coherent doctrine that can establish a synthesis between these apparent contradictons? That is the essential question raised by this book.

PART II

DE GAULLE AND FRENCH POLITICS—CIRCUMSTANCES AND STRATEGY

CHAPTER I

The Circumstances

How did a seditious general of June, 1940, turn into the authoritarian leader of state of 1966? What were the ways he chose and what were the obstacles? In a life both incredible and exceptional, what part was played by circumstances which provoked and guided De Gaulle's actions, and what part was played by his own strategy which, after many mishaps, led him to his final goal?

Nothing is more conducive to an exceptional political destiny than a world in ferment, a humiliated country in turmoil. Lenin benefited from the Czar's helplessness in solving Russia's social problems and those caused by the First World War. Hitler knew how to capitalize on Germany's woes after the Treaty of Versailles. Less brutally and less consciously, De Gaulle was helped in his rise to power by the weakness of France and by the confused state of its politics, as well as by the stiffening of the joints that overcame the democracies paralyzed by totalitarianism.

De Gaulle appeared in French history at a time when France, for specific reasons, was undergoing a fearsome process of aging and sclerosis. Twice he pulled the country back onto its feet. In the future he may provoke the necessary leap forward that will be his glory, whatever his past faults and mistakes.

For whether we like it or not, De Gaulle has come to be accepted as the living symbol of French greatness. With exceptional lucidity he has developed a policy that is practical

83

for our time. Unfortunately, pettiness and grudges dog that policy, so that it creates strife rather than unity, and blind hatreds as well as wild enthusiasms. Also, whether we like it or not De Gaulle undoubtedly stands for one of the West's last chances to adopt a program of healthy change, although, again unfortunately, he himself has not escaped the nationalism of the past.

This greatness and hope for the future appeared in a nation that, only ten years previously, had seemed the new Sick Man of Europe and often the laughingstock of the world.

After Two World Wars

One and a half million Frenchmen were killed during the First World War, between 1914 and 1918. The youngest and most active tenth of the adult male population was simply erased. And this happened in a country where, for nearly forty years, births had had the greatest difficulty in keeping pace with deaths. Over two million men were taken prisoner during the Second World War, between 1940 and 1945. Again the most active and youngest tenth of the adult male population was for a long time removed from the homeland. These figures do not include those men killed during the Second World War. There were 100,000 deaths during the French campaign of 1940 alone. It was, proportionate to the time it lasted, more costly in human lives than all the other campaigns later fought by the Anglo-Saxon Allies. Then there were those killed in the Resistance, by deportation, in Tunisia, and during the Liberation. The total of French dead reaches nearly 650,000. By 1945, France was totally exhausted, bled by two world wars. The country suffered from all the complexes and traumas brought on by anemia and debility.

When Socialist leader Léon Blum returned from deportation in May, 1945, he described France in terms full of sadness and truth:

"Ever since I arrived on French soil again, eight days ago, I must admit that I have been full of disappointment and anxiety for my country. I did not find what I was expecting. . . . I do not have the impression that France has returned to normal yet. I do not have the feeling that anything in the country is functioning normally yet.

"I get the impression of a tired, nonchalant, and lazy sort of convalescence completely open to every kind of infection. We will have to fight that with all our might. We will have to check it and put it right."

That was precisely what De Gaulle thought of as his own historic task between 1940 and 1946.

When Léon Blum wrote the remarks quoted above, and De Gaulle was still the leader of a nation at last freed again, what was the state of affairs in France? In a period of thirty years, France had known ten years of war, four years of occupation, governments by the Popular Front (Léon Blum and Daladier) and by the extreme right wing (Pétain), attempts at subversion (in February, 1934, and September, 1944) coming from two extremist camps and often supported by the center. Since 1934, France had gotten herself into the disastrous habit of being divided into two rival factions, each of which increasingly suspected the patriotism of the other. The days of February, 1934, of the Popular Front of 1936, of Munich in 1938, of Vichy, of dissidence and the Resistance from 1940 to 1944, and of the purges of 1945, successively split France's unity more and more irremediably. Finally the division was even deeper than it had been at the end of the previous century, when the debate over that tame Dreyfus Affair had (to the credit of that generation) split the country. Taking into account the unborn, France lost four million inhabitants during two wars, two-thirds of whom would have been in the prime of life by 1945. Economically, France suffered four years of acute inflation, nine years of crisis, and two four-year periods of illusory and temporary prosperity.

It was a country divided and torn, that had grown old and was living through all the failings of old age: impotence, nostalgia, fondness of a false security as long as it denied the need for any risk or initiative.

Its foreign policy was one of false security. Between the two world wars the whole arsenal of pacts and treaties with the countries of Central Europe, artificially created in the first place and threatened from within, turned out to be only scraps of paper. Hitler's first brutal assault would tear them up, and France was not even able to retaliate.

Its military strategy was also one of false security. The Maginot Line was reputedly impregnable, and this gave France peace of mind at having a "comprehensive insurance policy." It would take less than a month of fighting to show its futility.

France's economic and financial life was falsely secure. A niggling and glutted capitalism had forgotten that the first duty of capitalism is to use capital in the production of wealth. When wealth is hoarded, it becomes neutralized.

Lastly, its electoral customs were based on finicky theories and constantly changing; they got further and further away from the realities of life, of facts, and of men.

THE REPUBLIC OF PARTIES

Because of a wish to define every nuance of opinion, the French steadily increased the number of political parties. In the United States, political leaders seek to impose their imprint on the two great parties, the Republican and the Democratic, but from within. In France, every politician of any importance who disagrees with the policy of his party founds a new one. Before the war of 1939, Marcel Déat and Adrien

Marquet, disapproving of the policy of the Socialist party, had created another, called the Neo-Socialist party. In the same way, Jacques Doriot, disagreeing with the Communists, set up the French Popular party (P.P.F.). Again, Colonel de la Rocque, a newcomer to political activity, founded the French Social party (P.S.F.), which was to supplant the older parties on the right wing, without—for all that—ending their lives. Similarly, after the Second World War the M.R.P. had to be formed to express the progressive feelings which sprang up in Catholic circles.

The dust of the political groups soon settled. Often their names had no meaning for the uninformed voter. The "Republicans of the left" were of the right wing, the Socialist Radicals were anything but socialists. Frontism, which gathered together non-Communists of the left, was represented by only one deputy. Each candidate at the elections would choose his label and ornament it with different letters of the alphabet.

Added to this there were ruptures, divisions, and schisms within the old parties. At the Tours congress in December, 1920, the Socialist party had burst open, dividing into the Communist party, which gave its allegiance to the Third International, and the French section of the Workers' International (S.F.I.O.), which was attached to the Second International.

What was true of the parties was equally true of the trade unions. Before the war of 1939 there were at least four unions of some importance. There was the Communist General Confederation of Workers (C.G.T.), the Socialist Workers' Force (C.G.T.-F.O.), which was more tolerable to employers' circles, the French Confederation of Christian Workers (C.F.T.C.), which was non-Marxist but radical, inspired in the beginning by the social action of the great reforming popes after Leo XIII, and finally, the independent trade unions, called independent, apparently because they were linked to employers' organizations. If they were independent from the Communist C.G.T., they were less so from the National Council of French Manufacturers.

Thus a worker who wished to belong to a trade union had a choice of membership; but usually he did not know how to choose. How could he, when he was surrounded by competing sirens, all chanting about their marvelous programs? As for the voter who wished to do his duty, he was confronted with an even wider range of choice. As the Third Republic continued on its way, the system of voter's ballot became so rambling as to approach the abstract.

Before the war of 1914, the constituency poll was king. Each Department contained a number of constituencies; from each of them only one deputy was elected. Since this deputy represented only a small area, he could make himself known during the actual campaign, if he was not known already. The voters knew their candidate and could decide from their personal impressions of him, their contacts with him, and their knowledge of his past activities. The constituency polls still maintained a semblance of humanity. Above all, the candidate could show off his qualities as a private citizen and as a statesman on a small stage that suited his stature. He could run an election campaign on his own resources, he belonged to any one party (and this was not essential) only to inform the voter of his opinions, he did not need political backing to raise funds for his campaign. The election campaign was like a sporting event, a competition of personalities, where the energy and the presence of a candidate led him to a victory or a defeat which he owed only to himself. Campaigns relied on the bedrock of direct political contact.

Doubtless the constituency poll could be condemned for its dependence on regional influences and parochial intrigues, where concern for special or local interests could prevail over great national problems. There was also the famous problem of the "leftovers." Suppose that, in one constituency, the

right-wing candidate received 51 per cent of the votes, and the
left-wing candidate had the remaining 49 per cent. Suppose
that much the same thing took place in all of the constituencies of a Department, and suppose, to simplify even further, that the same breakdown existed in all the Departments
of the nation. The result would be that 49 per cent of the
French population would not be represented in Parliament.
This extreme case was certainly unlikely, but for people
obsessed with formal logic and arithmetical niceties (as the
promoters of electoral systems often are), probability counts
little in the face of abstraction. For them, every specific case is
too often only the exception pretending to be the rule. And
so, to right the theoretical inconveniences of the constituency
poll, proportional representation and ballot lists were invented. After World War II these were adapted to the Department or to an important fragment of the Department.
From that time on, when each voter placed in the urn the
precious voting paper—which his ancestors had won in battle
—he could be almost certain that it would not be in vain. If
his vote did not help to form a majority, at least it would be
added to a minority which would have its representatives and
its say in the affairs of state.

But would that say be the voter's? Would it be a say
dictated by his knowledge of the facts or urban or national
life? He had, after all, only supported the nominees of a party.
His vote was merely the echo of political decisions made at
party headquarters by a central directing committee whose
preoccupations would be of a different nature from those of
the various regions. In this way, the voter came to feel
alienated from his ballot, alienated from the mandate given
to the elected candidate.

With the ballot lists, the deputy owed his success to his
party and not to his personal standing in the constituency
which he was to represent. The essential part of the election
took place before the campaign, in the course of hidden and

often sordid intrigues at party headquarters, where a candidate had to be high on the list drawn up in national party centers. Compromises were useful, concessions necessary, and bootlicking profitable; the first virtue of a politician was his ability to convey platitudes. Servility was a must for any man who presumed to represent his district or to govern his country.

Confusion was soon added to servility. For in 1951, right in the middle of the deadlock over colonial policy in Indochina, in the midst of total domestic turmoil, Parliament devised yet another voting method. This method—so Parliament said and perhaps even believed—would insure governmental stability and the formation of majorities. It was the system of "pairing." Before elections, the parties decided who would form a coalition once the results were in. This was a convenient way for them to obtain an overall majority and win all the seats in the main elections; they could divide them later at their opponents' expense. From this time on, a candidate had to agree to be obedient and docile not only to his own party, but also to the parties which would be "paired" with his in order to win the election. If, for example, the candidate belonged to the Radical party and endorsed free enterprise, he had to promise to support nationalization to win Socialist backing for the secondary elections. And the opposite held true. The Socialists—those bottom-price Marxists—had to promise that they would back the Radicals' economic liberalism. If, as a Radical, the candidate supported secular education, he had to promise not to interfere with parochial schools, in order to get the backing of the M.R.P., and the M.R.P., the "party of faith," had to associate with, or at least not oppose, the anti-clerical cult of the Radicals.

Under the guise of insuring an efficient political system, paralysis followed; under the guise of insuring the unification of parties, each of them was rendered impotent; under the guise of guaranteeing governmental stability——but enough, the facts speak for themselves. This is the first argument against the electoral system which generates what De Gaulle calls the "regime of the parties." Its errors all take place before a deputy arrives at the Palais Bourbon.

The second argument against the electoral system is directed at the functioning of the newly-elected assembly in Parliament from the beginning of each session. If these badly-chosen deputies wish to preserve their chances of winning in the next election, they must obviously follow their party's orders. Because of some fatal flaw in the working of groups of politicians, however, each party ignores the fact that it may be only one among twenty, with infinitesimal power. It finds itself forced to act as though it were the sole party, or at least the government party. To become the majority party, or at least to belong to the majority party, is every party's vocation. If the election results do not allow it to show its true superiority, the party will achieve this later through backstairs intrigue. The aim of such intrigue is to share in the government, with one or several leading party members in the ministry.

And so, each party wants to be the party in power. It carries on intrigues to attain this end. It is forced to make a merry-go-round of the places in the Cabinet in order to strengthen its position. If four coalition governments follow each other in one year, there are four times as many chances to be a minister than in only one government lasting four times as long. The goal of parliamentary life, therefore, ceases to be the running of a government which expresses the permanent interests of a nation, and becomes instead the juggling of Cabinets, which expresses party interests from day to day.

This system could be compared to a burial club. The club's sole function is to guarantee the last rites of its members. It is a great occasion when one of them dies. All attend in their customary black outfits. Eyes are wet, but glances shine with satisfaction. At last, the club's function is being fulfilled. It is doing its duty.

When a minister of the Fourth Republic was being buried, the public galleries were filled, the benches were all occupied, and the corridors abuzz. France, in all this, acted the part of pallbearer. It received the condolences of foreign nations, although not of its citizens.

All this increased the alienation of voters. Political centralization, which concentrated the whole life of a nation in the back offices of Paris, left the running of the whole country in the hands of the same men. This is what De Gaulle took steps to end.

Without admitting it France was waiting, from 1946 to 1958, for the return of the man of June 18, 1940. De Gaulle's first brief appearance in power had shown the nation his exceptional merit without revealing his faults. France believed that he would cure the evils of the "regime of the parties."

The Third Republic, between the two wars, lasted twenty-two years; in other words, twice as long as the Fourth Republic, not counting De Gaulle. In that period, it "gobbled up" sixteen heads of government. Following is a list of their names; many of them deserve a place in history:

Alexandre Millerand, Georges Leygues, Aristide Briand, Raymond Poincaré, Édouard Herriot, Paul Painlevé, André Tardieu, Camille Chautemps, Pierre Laval, Joseph Paul-Boncour, Édouard Daladier, Albert Sarraut, Gaston Doumergue, Pierre Étienne Flandin, Léon Blum, Paul Reynaud.

In half that time, the Fourth Republic "gobbled up" fifteen leaders. Among them were some newcomers, whose names are already fading in the memories of their contemporaries: Félix Gouin, Georges Bidault, Léon Blum, Paul Ramadier, Robert Schuman, André Marie, Henri Queuille, René Pleven, Edgar Faure, Antoine Pinay, René Mayer, Félix Gaillard, Joseph Laniel, Bourgès-Maunoury, Pierre Pflimlin. As Cyrano said, "How beautiful! All those names, and not one will die!"

As for mere ministers, how can we recall them all? Their number is ten times that of the heads of government. In fact, on the average one deputy in five was in the Cabinet at some time or other.

From one Honors List to another, what a decline is there! From Édouard Herriot to Gaillard, poor Radical party! From Jean Jaurès to Félix Gouin, unlucky S.F.I.O.! From Flandin to Joseph Laniel, pitiful Independents! Yet these newcomers were not totally lacking in good qualities. During this period of impotence and sclerosis, France managed to produce, as she always has, vigorous and intelligent men with remarkable personalities, who were perfectly capable of running public affairs. But the party system, justly stigmatized by De Gaulle, prevented them from developing their powers. It nullified and finally eliminated them. Gaullist criticism of the parties seems justified.

But enough of theory, and back to fact, with the example of three contemporary statesmen who were made impotent by proportional representation and the "pairing" system— Mendès-France, Guy Mollet, and Jacques Soustelle. All of them represented France on the international scene, and all fully deserved to do so.

PIERRE MENDÈS-FRANCE, A RADICAL

One winter night, about forty years ago, the intern on duty at Cochin Hospital in Paris saw two young men come in with swollen faces. They were law students, members of a "University League of Republican and Social Action." They were returning from a public meeting which had been broken up by elements of the extreme right wing. One of the students on the speakers' platform had tried for two hours to quell the uproar. He had to be dragged down bodily by his enemies before they could force him to stop talking.

Student brawls were common at a time when the ruling left-wing coalition provoked noisy reactions from the monarchist rowdies. The intern recommended stitches and asked the two young men if they could afford to pay the regular fee. The two patients hesitated. Their students' wallets were not exactly bulging that evening. "We can pay in principle," they answered, "but it depends on the price." The amused intern asked them to pay two francs each, and put stitches in the two faces. One of those faces was destined to become well known.

This was not the first fight of Pierre Mendès-France. A fractured nose, still evident, testifies to that. The responsibility lay in his pugnacious nature, which he had had from childhood. He also had passionate convictions, stubborn opinions, and absolute confidence in his own destiny. During his university days, this budding politician told his fellow students: "When I'm twenty-five I shall be a deputy, and when I'm thirty-five I shall be a minister." They found this boast perfectly natural when they considered the young man's capacity for work, his lucidity, and his courage. In fact, as Pierre Mendès-France was born on January 11, 1907, the first of his predictions was fulfilled exactly in 1932. And the second was fulfilled in 1938, four years in advance of his prediction.

Thirty years after this episode Mendès-France led another brawl, from the floor of the National Assembly. The face that had once been sharp and angular had filled out, but the look from below the heavy eyelids was the same. He had served under Léon Blum in 1938 and under De Gaulle in 1944 and 1945; he had been Mayor of Louviers and President of the General Council of the Eure; he had won fame and a seat in Parliament after a bandwagon campaign in the Napoleonic style; he had become an expert on economic and financial questions, and one of the most heard—if not heeded—Members of Parliament; but none of these things had altered the frankness of his speech or had cooled his ardor. On the contrary, that summer in 1954, while the war in Indochina was pressing on to disaster, Mendès-France seemed to have redoubled his vigor. Until that time he had been involved mainly in economic and financial questions, but now he attacked political problems on all fronts, those of Europe and Indochina and North Africa. His range as an orator expanded as he dealt with more problems. The worse the problems became, the greater became his eloquence. He made the walls of the National Assembly ring with his anger. Such vehemence in politics had gradually been forgotten by Parliament.

In his speech on June 9, 1954, he did not mince his words to Georges Bidault, Minister of Foreign Affairs, with whose Indochina policy he vehemently disagreed.

"We find ourselves faced with a government whose lack of foresight has been obvious for years. This Cabinet has been noted, more recently, for its impulsiveness, its irrationality and continual contradictions."

Georges Bidault: "Thank you."

Pierre Mendès-France: "That thank-you was long overdue. France has not deserved this. France does not want this to go on much longer. All you who speak in her name, you representatives of the people, you must hear her voice at last, her anguish, her will, her demand for redress!"

Then he clarified his remarks. In doing so, he oddly anticipated what De Gaulle was to tell the United States in 1964 about the tragedy of Indochina:

"There is only one solution, and you will come around to it. It is a difficult solution, a painful solution, a cruel solution, and, in some respects, an unjust one. The solution is to open direct negotiations.

"Show the Vietnamese people that they can have peace

and independence, that they can receive it from us and not from Moscow and Peking. That is the very best investment we can make."

Mendès-France became Prime Minister four days later. To achieve his goal he used a tone and slogans which anticipated by four years De Gaulle's return to power from his quiet retreat at Colombey. Yet the great similarity in their ideas did not bring about an understanding between the two men.

One of the reasons is that Mendès-France is like the character of Molière's *Le Misanthrope:*

> . . . And he shall fight his own true convictions,
> As soon as he hears them in another's mouth!

Mendès-France was allergic to any collaboration between himself and anyone who surpassed or equaled him. He would do his best each time to conceal this under pretext of dogma or principle, but this fault nonetheless seems to stem from a neurosis.

Another reason is that at the time of De Gaulle's return to power, Mendès-France had long since ceased to be the head of the government. The sting of this failure would not have allowed him to join another.

Mendès-France failed because of two political mistakes, though the first of them was unavoidable. He erred first in becoming a member of one party, but even more serious was his choice of the most conformist of parties, the one most typical of the parliamentary faults of the Third and the Fourth Republics. How could he have expected that party to carry out a policy of reform that approached revolution—in the best sense of the word? Haphazardly—though perhaps understandably in view of his past—Mendès-France early on became a member of the Radical and the Radical-Socialist parties, which had absolutely nothing radical or socialist about them.

On February 3, 1955, after seven months and eighteen days

in power, he was forced to judge the consequences of his mistake. On the eve of his overthrow, he was on the rostrum to answer his opponents, the chief of whom was in his own party. He spoke in an even tone of voice, using only the eloquence of his convictions and of his pent-up anger. From time to time, in the same tone, he would throw out a barb that would lacerate one or another of his "dear colleagues."

"The time has not yet come for the ass to kick," he threw out at René Mayer, one of his Radical colleagues leading the assault against him. Unused to insults, the Assembly reacted. Booing drowned the speaker's voice.

Mendès-France stopped talking while the uproar went on, and drank a mouthful of milk, that bucolic drink which he favored in place of the traditional glass of water. When calm was restored, he repeated in the same even tone, to make sure he was understood, the words which had unleashed the uproar: "As I was saying, it is not yet time for the ass to kick." The Assembly was struck dumb, but it went its way, and so, unfortunately, did Mendès-France. He wound up his speech with a condemnation of "politics." Then he corrected himself and specified "odious politics." "Odious politics"? What did he mean, if not the politicking of the parties, the politicking of his own party, where the intrigue had begun that eventually led to his downfall?

When the vote of "no confidence" was taken and Mendès-France was overthrown, he did not go immediately to the Élysée to hand in his resignation, as so many Prime Ministers had done before him when they were faced with a minority government. Instead, he remained in the chair and tried to give a last address. He was not speaking to the deputies of a noisy Parliament, but above the heads of those who were calling him a "fascist" to public opinion, to the nation, to France. It was as though Mendès-France at that moment were setting the precedent which would lead De Gaulle to use the referendum.

It does not matter whether this was Gaullism before De Gaulle or Gaullism against De Gaulle. It was an inconsequential Gaullism which had let itself fall into the snare of the party system.

GUY MOLLET, A SOCIALIST

After Pierre Mendès-France, who struggled but finally succumbed to the party system, came Guy Mollet who was at home in it and who tried to use it. He might fail, but he had accepted the rules of a game which he thought he could win.

Mollet, the present Secretary General of the Socialist party (S.F.I.O.), is a born secretary general, a man born to be a secretary general the way others are born to be presidents of the Republic, princes of the Church, lawyers, admirals, or policemen. He holds the levers of command and, in all likelihood, also pulls the strings. He is a typical example of that bygone period of political life when everything was organized, rationalized, and administered, the control extending even to the party ideology, creating the drive of the party militants and especially the revolutionary spirit.

In the Paris office of the Cité Malesherbes, where he spends three-fifths of his active life at a plain businessman's table, Guy Mollet is surrounded by the portraits of those who have inspired the thinking or the deeds of his party, his predecessors or precursors, after a fashion. The most distant of his ancestors, "the great ancestor," cast in bronze, is one whom Mollet frequently quotes, Maximilien de Robespierre. Certain catchwords of the great Revolution sometimes crop up in Guy Mollet's speeches. "No one who is against the Revolution is right," the agitators of 1792 used to say; "no one who is against the party is right," the present party secretary echoes in a minor key. On the walls are the ideologists, looking down in disdain upon the callow men of our age. Karl Marx, Jaurès, Bracke Desrousseaux, a professor who died about ten years ago at ninety and who divided his time between editing the classics and inspiring the party—such is the ideological group which hears the ringing of telephones and the sound of typewriters, which watches over the meetings of party chiefs, and which receives the regional and foreign delegates of the party. In this nerve center of the party machine only one portrait, a more recent portrait, seems a little out of place. It is that of a beardless, mustached Léon Blum, the man who in *L'Échelle Humaine* tried to humanize Marxism. What would Blum think if he heard Guy Mollet define him as "Léon Blum, who knew where he was going but did not know how to get there?" Guy Mollet could say of himself, however, that he knows how to get where his party is already going. His route does not depend on him, but on the party as a whole.

He loves his party as De Gaulle loves France. It serves as an ideal to which he can devote himself, as a support, as a pedestal, and sometimes as an alibi. It is a left-wing party of "good comrades," people who have believed, ever since Jean-Jacques Rousseau, that human nature is good and that society corrupts it. These same people have believed since 1848 in social justice, in democracy, and in work. They have believed since Karl Marx in the class struggle. And they have believed in the separation of church and state since Sinai.

Of working-class origins, the son of a weaver and a concierge, Mollet had to work hard to reach his present position. He has known all the setbacks of life; he has surmounted all its obstacles. His father died of wounds received during the First World War. Young Guy, ward of his country, won a scholarship that enabled him to attend the *lycée* at a time when it was not yet free, and then to go on to higher education. Still, the cost was great—in effort, in envy, and in rebuffs. He began at the lowest rung of the ladder, as a boarding-school teacher, or junior master. The trade-unionist newspaper in which he published his first articles was called "Le Petit Chose"—a title which showed the hopelessness of these petty educators. Mollet's signature did not often appear in this paper, because the hardworking teacher wrote, at the age of eighteen and childless, under the pseudonym, "A family man." He needed compensation for his past. After getting his "license" he became an assistant professor at Arras. At the same time he became party secretary of a union for the first time, the supplementary teachers' union of the Pas-de-Calais region. The primary teachers' union was reserved for full professors.

His military career and the 1940 campaign were to provide him with more trials and more opportunities for revolt. Wounded, then made prisoner, he overcame his misery and his boredom by teaching English grammar to his comrades in the P.O.W. camp, using a phonetic method that he was to introduce in French universities. Repatriated because of his extensive wounds, he joined the Resistance and became one of the leaders responsible for the Civil and Military Organization (O.C.M.). He barely escaped the Gestapo and had to hide in Paris, then in the Yonne region, then in Normandy. He was there at the time of the Liberation, among an F.F.I. (*Forces Françaises de l'Intérieur*) group in a pocket at Falaise, and soon thereafter became secretary to the Regional Committee of the Liberation in Arras. It was his first step on the road that finally led him to choose the role of secretary of the Socialist party.

All the trials survived, both as a civilian and as a soldier, all the grudges he felt as a second-class instructor or as a fighter without a uniform in a humiliated country, all these risks and rebellions helped forge him for the job which suited him—the party secretaryship of an aggressive organization.

At a time when teachers' unions were forbidden, and only picked people were allowed to organize state employees, Guy Mollet, alias "a family man," defied the government by illegally creating and running one of those famous secondary unions that were the most vindictive and militant ones of all.

And he paid the price. At the beginning of his career in 1923 at Lisieux, he lasted as a boarding-school teacher for only twelve days. It was at the time when Henri Chéron, senator, mayor, and minister, forbade state employees to unionize. One hundred of them got together and unanimously decided to send their visiting cards to His Excellency, "with an expression of their deepest contempt." Ninety-eight "turned chicken"; only two were bold enough to keep the appointment. Guy Mollet was one of these two, and as a disciplinary measure he was transferred to Le Hâvre.

The early militant became a politician, a Member of Parliament, a minister, the president of a commission, and Prime Minister. The congresses which had once only heard debates on salaries and temporary posts were replaced by congresses which heard debates on the future of France and of Europe. All the same, from his early struggles to his most important duties, Guy Mollet has always remained something of a unionist and a petty teacher. This is what ties him to his job. In his seat and base, the Pas-de-Calais union where he is party secretary, he is called by his Christian name. Everyone greets him affectionately; he talks with the miners and shows himself to be a proletarian like them. At the party offices in the Cité Malesherbes in Paris he is surrounded by militant devotees, either helpers or staff, who make sure he gets rest, who look after his work, who respond to the affection as well as to the orders of the boss. The discipline is friendly, the zeal comradely.

Mollet echoes at the summit the decisions made at the grassroots. These decisions do not surprise him, for he has either brought them to life or registered their birth. He gets votes on motions prepared at the Cité Malesherbes; he knows their terms in detail. Since the congress of August, 1946, which demoted Daniel Mayer to the advantage of Guy Mollet, no congress has been scandalous enough to refuse its moral support to its leader. Has anyone ever seen a party in session, with all its unions assembled, that did not raise a forest of hands for the motions proposed by its party secretary?

That then is democracy, and a republic of political parties, a subtle game of boomerangs thrown between summit and grassroots, between party secretary and the mass of members. This was how, during the Fourth Republic before De Gaulle came to power, domestic policy was evolved. Under a mask of universal and direct suffrage, politics had again become a question of bloc voting at various levels. It was exactly the same system that had existed during the Restoration or the July Monarchy.

Guy Mollet's secret lies in this method of using his party. Old fox that he is, he doubtless has his tricks for channeling the undercurrents that move the mass of the party. But he is forbidden to oppose them face to face. He has doubtless had to backtrack, like any other man, in a way that must have made Robespierre blush from the top of the mantelpiece. But these recantations, which are the bread of politicians, were rarely gratuitous or voluntary. For the most part, they showed the way the party was going.

In order to get the party secretaryship at a time when the S.F.I.O. was racked by crisis and was beginning to feel disappointed after the Liberation, Mollet used the grudges of the party by siding with the extreme left wing. Thus he gained the support of Trotskyite elements and even Communist sympathizers. It was a dangerous game, which certainly went against the grain of his deepest convictions. But he would not hesitate to play the same game again each time the grassroots showed too strong an inclination to unite with those who took orders from Moscow. That was clear in 1964.

He had supported the European Defense Community, and he had condemned De Gaulle's concept of Europe and his refusal to give up any part of national sovereignty. Yet he himself had often shifted his ground on this subject, prompted by the congress at Arras or near Paris. In the beginning, he voted against and wanted to speak violently against the rearmament of Germany within the E.D.C. framework. An undercurrent in the party, evident in a decision of the Central Committee, made him change course. On the speaker's platform he spoke up for the new trend in his party and against his previous convictions. It is too easy to call these actions mere opportunism. It is more a question of the change of course a party leader must make. He has to change to suit the party's needs and demands, its prejudices and its patterns. "They have chosen me as leader. That is why I follow them."

Before one session of a party congress at Arras began, I had a private conversation with Guy Mollet in which he pointed out that there was every reason for a political coalition between his party and the M.R.P. He wished, for the sake of French political stability, that such an agreement could be reached. When the congress began, the ordinary party members on the speaker's platform came out with some of the usual fine phrases against the M.R.P., about its receiving its orders from Rome. At the first recess, stunned, I went to find Guy Mollet: "But where are we?" I asked. "What age is this? What country? What place? How can a speech of miserable slogans left over from Madame Bovary's chemist, Monsieur Homais, get such applause? . . . But you, Guy Mollet, can you agree with it?"

"Of course not," he answered, "but we can do nothing. . . . These prejudices which are so out-of-date, these grudges which hurt national unity so much at a time when more urgent questions compel our attention, are the result of local and historical peculiarities of the Pas-de-Calais. I can do nothing about them. My good comrades remember being told by their fathers or their grandfathers that, in their great-grandfathers' days, no man could be taken on at the mine without showing that he had been to confession. . . . Of course, this practice was abolished a long time ago. But it's still left its mark on them. And if I didn't take it into account, I'd be thrown out at once."

On that note, Guy Mollet proudly climbed onto the speaker's platform again. He wanted to explain why, as mayor of Arras, he would have to refuse a grant to a Catholic school. This party game debases politics, and at various levels it affects the great political decisions of the nation and the world. De Gaulle and the Gaullists had to try to free themselves from it.

JACQUES SOUSTELLE, A GAULLIST

One man, Jacques Soustelle, had every quality needed for success. He was the most committed and the most dedicated of the Gaullists. By training and by temperament he felt distaste for the policies of the Members of Parliament, he disliked the dictates of the party system, and inspired by De Gaulle, he seemed to be the man to rid France of the parties. If he failed, who could succeed?

His father was a mechanic and his mother, too, had worked at Villeurbanne, near Lyons. His ancestors were Protestants who had suffered for their faith, and perhaps they inspired him to refuse an easy life. Though nothing in his early days pointed to a brilliant career, he was noticed by his elementary-school teacher, who persuaded his parents to allow their son to continue his studies and encouraged him to get a scholarship. At the age of seventeen, he was the top student admitted to the École Normale Supérieure; he had an advanced degree in philosophy at the age of twenty; and by the time he was twenty-five, he had a doctorate and was Vice-Director at the Musée de l'Homme. It was a flamboyant and supremely successful career, not only because of the speed at which he forged ahead, but also because of the obstacles in his path.

Jacques Soustelle left erudite works based on books in

libraries to other academics. He needed larger horizons and field work. He had hardly gotten his advanced degree before he set off for Mexico to prepare a thesis on the Otomis, a small people of the high plateaus, and on the Lacandons, a dying branch of the Mayan tribes, on the border between Guatemala and Mexico. In 1932, he went some hundreds of miles through barren countryside in the interior and at high altitudes to witness an Otomi festival. On his return to France in 1938, he presented a doctoral thesis which is still the definitive work on the Otomi-Dame tribe of Central Mexico.

Time spent in civilizations so different from the French were a bad preparation for the subtleties and the maneuvers of European life. The Aztec mind is more intuitive and less rational than the European. They believe that "good luck" accompanies every human being, and that if his good luck goes to sleep, he becomes prey to every misfortune. Jacques Soustelle is the kind of man who keeps his good luck awake and who believes more in intuition than in logic—in other words he is exactly the kind of man who feels the closest ties with the Otomis. Their legends, like the one of the creation of the sun and the moon, exalt courage. "The gods realized with terror that the two heavenly bodies did not move. They remained motionless above the horizon, burning the world with their fire. It was because they were dead and needed blood to bring them back to life. And so the gods decided to sacrifice themselves. 'Let us all die,' they said. 'Let us bring the sun back to life again by our death.' One of them, Eecatl, as God of the Wind, chose the task of killing them all. . . . And then, above the sacrificed gods, drawing life from their death, the sun and the moon began their course through the sky."

To have known these myths and to have known also the civilizations which gave birth to them influenced the historian in Soustelle and made him allergic to the political game. The history that Soustelle studied had no connection with the petty sequence of events which, in peaceful times, characterizes the game of politics. The Mayan people, whose history Soustelle rediscovered, were a flourishing nation, civilized and prosperous till the day the Spaniards landed in the New World and quickly destroyed them.

As a politician, Soustelle seems to have kept a sense of history which tells him that catastrophe is always possible. Men may concentrate their will power on fighting tragedy and either overcome it or succumb to it. The heavenly bodies may stop, but men can start them again on their course. "There are," he has said, "moments in the existence of a people when its destiny seems to hesitate. In these rare moments of distress and greatness, the balance on the scale trembles. If the will of a man is added to one of the scales the arm tilts, imperceptibly even, toward life or toward death." Such moments occurred not only among the Mayas. In our days, and even in France, destiny seemed to hesitate. And Soustelle was to see it hesitate often.

Metaphorically speaking, commonplace politicians guide themselves by a wind gauge, following the way the wind is blowing. The instrument that would better suit Soustelle's character is the seismograph, which measures the extent of earthquakes. As he listens attentively to the deep movements of the soil and of history, Soustelle senses potential catastrophes that can bring utter ruin to our civilization. There is something apocalyptic about his political concepts.

This was the feeling behind his deep commitment to one of the few men who, in his eyes, stood for the nation's destiny. While many time-servers were interested chiefly in their own careers and were loyal to De Gaulle only when his chances looked good, Soustelle was always seduced by his chosen leader. He admired the bearing and the stature that made De Gaulle stand above petty squabbles; he admired the forthright sense of French destiny that linked him to the great days of national history. Soustelle remained devoted to him until 1958, or, rather, remained devoted to the image that he had of him.

"The temporary immortality," he wrote, "that the memory of nations grants to certain names is never so much connected with utility as with greatness. In the contest between great men, Napoleon always comes before Parmentier. This may be regretted; but perhaps it is so because our species is bored, and it recognizes instinctively the rare actions that light up its drab life with the flash of free will." And in a phrase with the ring of a confession or a manifesto, he praised "the pure joy that a man in politics feels when he sacrifices the present for what he considers the essential."

In fact, for Soustelle to have reached the point where he could write these words, he must have veered, like so many others, toward politics. And like so many others, he must have been ready to use the politics of his age, the politics of the party system. This strange alteration in him was due to De Gaulle, whose maneuvers he followed.

In 1942, during the war, Soustelle first served in De Gaulle's government as National Commissioner at the Information Bureau. Then in 1943, in Algiers, he acted as Director General of the Special Services.

After the Liberation, Soustelle served in Bordeaux as Commissioner of the Republic, as super-prefect, and later as deputy from Mayenne at the First Consultative Assembly, where he presented the General's point of view. On May 30, 1945, he became Minister of Information in De Gaulle's government, and on October 20, Colonial Minister.

In January, 1946, when De Gaulle left power, Soustelle also handed in his resignation. He seemed ready to give up his career in politics, which the parties were beginning to infiltrate and dominate again. Unfortunately, a double stroke of fate prevented him from doing so. The first stroke was that De Gaulle, in his struggle against the party system, began by trying to turn it to his own advantage. In 1947, he created the *Rassemblement du Peuple Français* (R.P.F.). In principle, this was not a party; but in Parliament and in the country, De Gaulle was eventually forced to play the party game, opposing or joining one or more of the parties, as necessary. The second stroke of fate was that Soustelle, the least corrupt of the incorruptibles, had to demonstrate his integrity by breaking with De Gaulle in the end. Soustelle, a committed Gaullist from the start, was chosen by the General as Party Secretary of the R.P.F. and as editor-in-chief of its newspaper, *Le Rassemblement*. Elected deputy from the Rhône in 1951, he became president of the parliamentary group that made up the Gaullist party. This group did not survive coalitions by other parties, and the General dissolved it on May 6, 1953.

But because of Algeria, Jacques Soustelle was not finished. For him and for De Gaulle, the Algerian war was the test of French vitality. "If Algeria were to be lost," Soustelle said in the National Assembly on March 3, 1956, "it would be like Sedan." Soustelle had spent the past two years as Governor General of Algeria, from January 26, 1955, to February 1, 1956. When he arrived in Algeria, he was threatened by the nationalists of Algiers who claimed that he was a convinced supporter of the federalist solution to the war, a plan hostile to integration of Algeria and France. "All those who feel national concern for preserving French Africa," a right-wing journalist wrote, "consider that the moment is ill chosen for appointing a Governor General in Algiers whose doctrines are so dangerous and reckless. Decked out in gold braid, he will probably justify our fears by trying out some hidden reform program, which could lead to a catastrophe." When Soustelle left Algeria, those who had attacked and insulted him were now in a frenzy of sorrow; they demonstrated to get him to stay. The same right-wing journalist then wrote about a short speech made by Soustelle on his departure: "We insist on publishing this remarkable text *in full*, without adding the least comment to or changing the least comma of the speech of this remarkable man."

What had occurred in the interval? Soustelle must have become aware of certain data concerning Algeria that he had not previously known, or else he had let himself be influenced by the unwise prophecy of De Gaulle, when he heard of Soustelle's appointment to Algiers: "It is you, Soustelle, who will be responsible before history if Algeria is abandoned."

Two years later, the two men split. Soustelle and De Gaulle were at loggerheads, a great misfortune for both of them. Disappointed by the parties and by the enemy of the parties, Soustelle had nowhere to turn but to rebellion against the man he had admired so much.

THE SLEEPING SICKNESS OF THE DEMOCRACIES

Just as De Gaulle opposed the party system in domestic politics, so his mission in foreign politics has been to react against the rigid thinking of the democracies, hypnotized and paralyzed by totalitarian powers for a quarter of a century.

On March 7, 1936, in violation of the Versailles Treaty, Hitler's German troops brutally reoccupied the Rhineland. Since that time, the political initiative, which the victorious democracies of 1918 used so poorly, has reverted to the dictatorships of the extreme right and the extreme left. For thirty years, the Western countries have confined themselves to fending off successive blows. Their attitude has alternated between that of frightened sheep rushing blindly into the slaughterhouse, and that of rams blindly butting each other with lowered horns.

In 1938, there was Hitler's invasion of Austria, followed by Munich. In 1939, the remnants of Czech and Slovak independence were suppressed in violation precisely of the Munich agreement signed a few months previously.

In April of the same year, Italy annexed Albania with less

difficulty than it had encountered in Ethiopia. There followed a pact of nonaggression between the U.S.S.R. and Germany, and less than a month later, the outbreak of World War II itself.

Even during the war, the dictators called the tune. Only their aggression provoked reaction. The U.S.S.R. attacked Finland on November 30, 1939, and put an end to its dogged resistance after a fight of three and a half months. Then the U.S.S.R. annexed the Baltic States, and still no one found anything to say.

Only after Russia had annexed the East European countries after the war, and after Chiang Kai-shek's China collapsed before that of Mao Tse-tung, did the democracies begin to act. Faced with all these provocations and changes and violations of agreements reached during the war, the democracies attempted to put up some opposition. At times they succeeded, but this does not alter the fact that it was the dictatorships which acted first, and it is the dictatorships which have kept the gains won by their own initiative.

American strength has, indeed, thwarted the progress of totalitarianism in key areas. It has succeeded in Korea and in Berlin, maintained in Formosa one outpost on a continent submerged by the tide of Red invasion, and doubtless the world has been very lucky that NATO gave the Western nations the chance to recover, thanks to American tanks, atomic weapons, and dollars.

But these have been defensive actions. Since 1945, as before 1939, the initiative has belonged to dictators, and though they are no longer the same ones, they are still without rival in their influence over the free nations and their power over the underdeveloped countries.

A dictatorship expelled the French from Indochina, took over North Vietnam and menaced South Vietnam; a dictatorship chased the British from Egypt, and another dictatorship took over in Havana. Country by country, the democracies try to resist the blows. Bit by bit, they repair the breaches. They retreat in order and sometimes prepare a few counterattacks.

Admittedly it was a victory to save Korea, to prevent France and Italy from going Communist, and to keep West Berlin. Admittedly it was useful to create a Common Market, although an ill-conceived and badly-prepared E.D.C. was, unfortunately, to hamstring its operation.

Despite these victories, any look at the map of the world shows the tide of totalitarianism creeping in; the democratic dykes are cracking. It is apparent that the democracies are using modern weapons to defend political systems from the last century. They continue to seem conservative and jaded when compared with the progressive dictatorships, who work so seductively on the underdeveloped countries.

The fault lies in the lack of imagination, inventiveness, and boldness of the free countries, and in the massive initiative of the dictatorships. The situation cannot last. The United States is reaching an impasse. It knows that, although its weapons are good, its strategy is bad and obsolete.

And now De Gaulle appears. He begins by breaking up the rigid patterns of diplomacy and getting in the way of vested interests. He takes initiatives that try not to ignore new conditions in the world. These initiatives may be bad, dangerous, and destructive. They may be rather partial, and they may be based on insecure policies. Perhaps, in the interest of doing something, he prefers devious moves to frontal attacks, encirclement to assault, and lies to frankness. Above all, he may run the risk of paying too much for what he gets.

Yet it is a fact that someone in the Free World is now taking some initiative. For although De Gaulle is authoritarian, he is no dictator. If he uses and twists the freedom of others to his own advantage, he does not suppress it. He is the first man from a Western, biblical tradition who has taken the initiative back from atheistic materialism.

He may be acting badly, he may not be successful, but at

least he has acted. He has stirred us up from our stagnation. The only thing to fear is that he may, at the same time, dig up the roots of our lives.

How did De Gaulle come to power, how did he remove from the hands of the nerveless the fearsome ability to act which, for better or worse, for life or death, he now controls— and with it the destiny of his country and his time?

De Gaulle's Strategy

A KIND OF CAESAR

In his fashion, De Gaulle is a kind of Caesar who could never take the first step across the Rubicon. Thus he is always changing direction unexpectedly, leaving in disarray those who have tried to follow him in the direction they think he has chosen. To their amazement, they find themselves suddenly alone, with De Gaulle already far away on a different road, going in a different direction altogether.

This has always been so. The way De Gaulle has behaved toward political parties all through his career will testify to it.

THE RUBICON OF THE PARTIES

From the very beginning, De Gaulle has disliked the political parties and wished he could do without them, for he has been unable to destroy or get around them. We know for certain that he was brought up in the monarchist tradition. One of my correspondents, an ex-member of Action Française and a founder of many provincial branches of the movement claims that he heard one of the leaders of Action Française— perhaps Maurras' secretary, Bernard de Vaulx, or the Count de Vésins—say that a young serving officer named Charles de Gaulle paid two visits to the rue de Rome within the space of a few days. De Gaulle wanted to interview Maurras and to express his "admiration" and his attachment to the monarchy.

These contacts with the Action Française were later denied; they do not appear in any of the biographies sanctioned by De Gaulle himself. They point to a time when the future General, impressed by Maurras' ideas, certainly opposed the action of the parliamentary parties. De Gaulle perhaps saw that the audience of the Action Française was not large enough to allow him to expound and succeed with his theories on the coming war. So he resigned himself, at a later stage, to try to convince the leaders of the parties.

One by one, he approached Members of Parliament on both sides. On the right he tried Le Cour Grandmaison; on the left, Philippe Serre, Marcel Déat, and Léo Lagrange. He furnished Paul Reynaud with the text of an amendment providing for the formation of an armored corps. Reynaud was to present it in Parliament. The amendment was brushed aside by the Minister of War, General Maurin, on March 15, 1935. When the Popular Front came to power in 1936, De Gaulle cherished the illusion that a revolutionary Cabinet would bring a little light into the skulls of the General Staff. He contacted Léon Blum, who had known of his ideas since March, 1935, but had not yet decided to use them.

FROM LÉON BLUM TO PAUL REYNAUD

"I beg everyone to realize," the leader of the Socialist party later wrote about this episode, "that if Colonel de Gaulle's ideas had won me and if Paul Reynaud's direct appeal had moved me, I was very far from being as absolutely sure as I was after the event. The facts had not yet declared their verdict. Discussion was open. Colonel de Gaulle's arguments were doubtless strong, but the objections to them were disturbing. . . ."

When Léon Blum reached power in 1936, he requested that De Gaulle come to see him. Two differing accounts remain of this interview.

I saw a man enter with calm, almost placid, assurance [Léon Blum wrote]. There was something gigantic about his size, his bearing, and his build. I am trying to put into words an impression that I have kept over the years. It was not only vivid, but it had a quality, a tone to it. And the truest thing I can find to say is that I felt, at first contact, that here was a man "all of a piece." He was all of a piece physically. Each of his gestures moved his whole body naturally. He was all of a piece in his moral character. The man who showed himself to me in this way, who stared at me so tranquilly, who spoke to me in his slow measured voice, could obviously not concern himself with more than one idea, one aim, one belief at a time. But when he had a belief, he had to give himself utterly to it, without considering any other factor. He could scarcely conceive that others would not surrender themselves fully to the conviction that possessed him. He bore no resemblance to the visionary inventor fascinated by his own idea. He cherished no chimera, no illusion. Rather, he had a trace, I will not say of discouragement nor even of weariness, but of disenchantment. He certainly had resolved to persevere in the task that he had undertaken for almost two years. There was no weakness of the will in his nature, no compromise. But he did not seem to believe in the possible success of his effort. . . . Clemenceau was the perfect example of such men, whose misanthropic, often scornful temperaments prevent them from believing in the use of an action—yet nothing can prevent them from acting, because to them action is a vital necessity. Colonel de Gaulle gave me the impression of belonging to that category. Our conversation was prolonged by me rather than by him. I think that he had come only to relieve his conscience of a duty . . . without expecting any positive result from it. I gave him to understand, before he left me, that I would find his presence on the staff of the Ministry of War a very good thing. The Colonel avoided this overture before I had even finished putting it into words. He declared, in a composed voice, that he had been assigned to begin the courses at the *Centre des Hautes Études Militaires,* and during that time he would not be able to take on any other post. On this note we parted, and in spite of all the troubles I had at the time, the meeting I have just described remained etched in my memory.*

De Gaulle described it in the following fashion:

Léon Blum warmly assured me of his interest in my ideas. "But," I said to him, "you have fought them in the past." "One's point of view changes when one becomes leader of a government," he answered. We spoke at first of what would happen if, as had to be expected, Hitler marched on Vienna, Prague, or Warsaw. "It's very simple," I pointed out. "Depending on the situation, we shall call up our active reserves or later mobilize our inactive reserves. And then, looking over the tops of our battlements, we shall watch passively while Europe is subjugated." "What!" Léon Blum cried out. "Would you have us send an expeditionary force to Austria, Bohemia, or Poland?" "No," I said. "But if the Wehrmacht advances along the Danube or the Elbe, why shouldn't we go along the Rhine? While they advance on the Vistula, why shouldn't we enter the Ruhr? In any case, the very fact that we would be capable of counterattack would doubtless prevent aggression. But our present system stops us from making a move." Recalling the declaration issued that morning by Leopold III, I pointed out that it was our lack of a selected armored corps and, consequently, our inferiority to the Germans which was costing us the Belgian alliance. The head of our government did not contest this, although he believed that Belgium's attitude was not based wholly on strategic reasons. "At any rate," he said, "our defensive front and our fortifications would protect our own territory." "Nothing is less certain," I replied. "In the future, the concentration of a sufficient mass of armor will be able to break through any defensive barrier in any given sector. Once the Germans have made a breach, they will be able to push a quick-moving Panzer group, backed by their air force, far behind our lines. If we have the same armored groups, we can still save everything. If not, all will be lost." The Prime Minister announced to me that the government . . . had decided to set aside . . . huge sums for national defense, and that an important part of it was to go for tanks and airplanes.

* Léon Blum, *Naissance de la IVᵉᵐᵉ Republique* (Paris: Albin Michel, 1958), p. 10.

I called his attention to the fact that nearly all of the planes they were planning to construct were designed to intercept, not to attack. As for the tanks, nine-tenths of them were of the Renault and Hotchkiss type of 1935, designed to support infantry warfare but not at all to form large, self-sufficient units. In any case, nobody was giving it any consideration. Our military set-up would remain what it was, then. The use of credits allotted to the war department was the concern of Monsieur Daladier and General Gamelin, the Prime Minister observed. "Without a doubt," I replied. "But allow me to think that national defense is the responsibility of the government." During our conversation, the telephone had rung ten times, drawing Monsieur Blum's attention to minor parliamentary or administrative questions. As I was taking my leave, while he was still on the telephone, he made a great gesture of weariness. "You see how easy it is for the head of a government to stick to the plan you have outlined," he said, "when he cannot even keep his mind on the same idea for five minutes!"*

Even if the General's account in his *Memoirs,* written nearly twenty years after the event, may seem to be something of an a posteriori demonstration of his lucidity and his gift for prophecy—for he is a man who, as we have seen, is not always very objective—Léon Blum does still confirm that De Gaulle judged the "system" not suited to the realization of his ideas. The Socialist Prime Minister had shown himself as a man of good will, but in spite of his revolutionary training he was absorbed in the parliamentary game and was bogged down by party maneuverings.

Disappointed by the left wing, De Gaulle had the brief illusion in March, 1940, during the "phony war," that he would succeed with the help of the right wing. On March 21, the government led by Daladier resigned, and Paul Reynaud took over. One of his first acts before he formed a ministry was to call De Gaulle back from the front in Lorraine. He gave him the job of drafting his first speech to the Chamber

---

* *The Complete War Memoirs of Charles de Gaulle* (New York: Simon and Schuster, 1959).

of Deputies. To De Gaulle, this seemed his long-awaited opportunity for using the regime to renovate France's military strategy and to avoid the disaster that was then imminent. Unfortunately, the game of parties began even before the Cabinet was formed. To win a majority, Reynaud had to include the Radicals, so he was forced to accept again as Minister of National Defense the same Daladier whose handling of affairs had brought on the crisis. In military matters Daladier had ideas that were diametrically opposed to those of Reynaud, in other words to those of De Gaulle. His presence guaranteed the continued existence of the strategy which Reynaud wished to change. Daladier opposed any post going to De Gaulle. "If De Gaulle comes here," he announced from his office at the rue Saint-Dominique, "I shall go out of this office, I shall go downstairs, and I shall telephone Reynaud to tell him to put De Gaulle in my place."

In return for this, Reynaud got his majority by one vote, and De Gaulle returned to the front. For the time being, he once again gave up the idea of using the parties to solve the nation's plight. Unable to turn aside the Rubicon, he was at last going to be forced to cross it.

JUNE 17 AND 18, 1940

This he did on June 17 and June 18, 1940, when he left French soil for good and delivered his first appeal over the B.B.C. for the continuation of the struggle.

In his *Memoirs* he gives a dramatic description of his feelings:

As I proceeded to speak these irrevocable words, I felt one life ending within me, the life I had led within the framework of a strong France and an indivisible army. At the age of forty-nine I was setting out on an adventure, as a man whom destiny was tossing out of his normal ways.*

* *Ibid.*

Yet these irrevocable words, which have since become the General's glory and France's honor, were hardly as irrevocable at the time as they now seem to be. A study of De Gaulle's actions after his speech seems to show again that his crossing of the Rubicon did not occur as simply and as deliberately as we are tempted to believe. He still hesitated over the role he was to play. He seemed ready, in the beginning, to follow the orders of a military leader with better qualifications than his own.

On June 19, he cabled General Noguès: "London, June 19, 1940. Am in London in direct and unofficial contact with the British government. Holding myself at your disposition, either to fight, or for any step that will seem useful to you." On June 20, he entrusted General Lelong, military attaché in London, with a letter for General Weygand asking him to take on the leadership of the rebels. "I believe I can tell you very simply, General, that I wish, for France's sake and for your own, that you may know how to and may be able to escape the disaster, reach overseas France, and continue the war. There is at present no armistice possible with honor."

These appeals remained unanswered, but they reveal that De Gaulle had not finally made up his mind. Even more significant is his answer of June 20 to the Pétain government's order from Bordeaux that he return to France. "General de Gaulle is ready to carry out the order to return sent by cable. But, in the absence of Colonel Rozoy, the [French military] mission can neither send a French airplane nor obtain a British airplane. General de Gaulle is going to make a personal request for an English airplane."

This text is clearly an unconditional acceptance of an order. Perhaps De Gaulle at that time still did not want to burn all his bridges. Henri Amouroux, in his remarkable book about June 18, 1940, has linked the contents of this cable to a letter sent to the same General Weygand.

General,

I have received your order to return to France, and I immediately inquired into the means of doing so. I have no intention, of course, of doing anything except serving in action.

I am thus thinking of coming before you within the next twenty-four hours, if, within that time, the act of capitulation has not been signed.

Amouroux rightly stresses the last sentence of the letter, which he says is the essential part: "if, within that time, the act of capitulation has not been signed." But this phrase does not occur in the telegram, in which no reservations are expressed and no conditions set for De Gaulle's return to France. Moreover, the telegram would certainly reach Weygand a long time before the letter, thus allowing De Gaulle a final chance to maneuver and to retrace his steps. Circumstances decided otherwise. This does not alter the fact that, very briefly, De Gaulle kept open a narrow escape route from his position of disobedience.

Soon De Gaulle gave up all alternatives and all desire to retrace his steps or to weaken his decision. He now found himself in a situation without precedent in French history, one which would still cause him to falter on occasion.

An unexpected political development took place during the months of June and July, 1940, after the disaster that ended the first phase of the war for France, for after seventy years of a Republic there was an authentic Restoration. It was a Restoration, if not of an actual monarchy, at least of its principles. All authority was concentrated in one man. The gulf between that sovereign authority, in the hands of a permanent monarch, and the power grabbed by a staff of chief clerks, servants of their country, ministers or senior civil servants, who were chosen and replaced by the unchanging chief of state, was immense.

The time was out of joint. Rival factions claimed they represented the nation; civil war raged within foreign war, between Vichy and London, Pétain and De Gaulle. This monarchist Restoration was thus split and ambivalent, having two "kings" at once, who fought, insulted, and canceled each other out completely.

ONE MONARCHY, TWO MONARCHS

In the first period at Vichy, until Laval's return to power in April, 1942, Pétain carried the monarchist principle to its furthest limit. "One day," Pierre Laval wrote at the beginning of Pétain's National Revolution, "I was fed up with his use of personal power. So I said to the Marshal, '*Monsieur le Maréchal*, are you aware of the extent of your powers?' 'No,' he answered. 'They are greater than those of Louis XIV,' I said, 'because Louis XIV had to submit his edicts to Parliament; you don't have to submit your constitutional acts to Parliament, because Parliament no longer exists.' 'That's true,' he replied."

In London, the monarch was De Gaulle. Since, in the early days of his rebellion, he had failed to bring over to his side Mandel, Reynaud, or any of the great leaders of the Third Republic, he began to run things all by himself. For him the radio appeal of June 18 set up a new and legitimate authority, a modern version of the Sacred Ampulla of Rheims.

There are further strange parallels between the two enemies, who both claimed to represent the continuity of government in a period of great crisis. Curiously enough, both of them would find themselves forced, at almost the same time, to alter the principle of monarchy and resign themselves to the restoration of party politics. Pétain took this significant step under Nazi pressure, especially after the occupation of the "Free Zone" in November, 1942, which allowed Laval to take over all power. The tables were turned. Political thinking took on a wholly new direction: real power would take precedence over mere authority. Henceforth, the Marshal was only a character actor, and he would soon abdicate all his rights.

The party men of the Third Republic again took up their places in the government: Cathala, Bonnefous, Grasset. And the government progressed toward the scrapping of the National Revolution and a last-ditch effort to install, at the end of the Occupation, a parliamentary regime in which the parties would play a role.

De Gaulle made his decision a few months later, in April, 1943. Until that time the General had paid little attention to the few Members of Parliament who had joined him in London. In his memoirs, Pierre Bloch describes De Gaulle's unenthusiastic reception of him. The General openly underlined the insignificance of the small parliamentary group which had been salvaged and which claimed to represent France. In fact, De Gaulle could very well have done without any parliamentary control. But in April, 1943, before leaving London for Algiers to take over the command of the French forces of the Resistance with Giraud, he received a letter from Léon Blum, then a prisoner at Bourrassol in France. "I take it for a fact," the ex-Prime Minister wrote, "that you have unreservedly stood by the principle of democracy. And I take for an unalterable fact that a democratic state—whatever its constitution and whatever part is played by the representatives of Parliament—cannot exist and may not even be a rational possibility without the existence of political parties. The organizers of the Resistance, who have left French soil to follow you, can in no way act as a substitute for these parties. . . ." De Gaulle must have taken this peremptory advice. He began to include the parties in his administration along with the forces of the Resistance.

And so Pétain and De Gaulle, the two men responsible for French politics during the time of the Occupation, both found themselves obliged to return to the party system. Though they were both hostile to it, and though they faced totally different situations, they returned to it for much the same reasons. For Pétain, whose time in office was running out and whose regime had no successor, this return to a system he would have liked to change had no grave or lasting consequences for his country. For De Gaulle, the return had consequences which still affect French life.

Apparently De Gaulle was not delighted with Léon Blum's letter, but he had to take it into account, if only to insure the unity of the Resistance. He had to be able to claim that he represented all of French opinion. As I have said before, in the provisional Consultative Assembly in Algiers, the first step in the rebirth of the parliamentary regime, the Assembly was hand-picked, not elected. It had no real power, except of consultation, and the political parties were hardly represented, compared to the Resistance movements. The 102 members of the Assembly consisted of 70 representatives of the Resistance, both metropolitan and rural, 12 general councilors of the liberated territories of North Africa, and only 20 ex-Members of Parliament. Of these, 5 were Socialists, 5 from the left-center (Radicals, members of the Republican Socialist Union, and Popular Democrats), 3 Communists, and 7 representatives of the center and the right.

For the time being, doubtless, the risks were limited. But in this Assembly made up chiefly of beginners in public life, the political experience of practiced politicians counted. Men like Gouin, Vincent Auriol, Henri Queuille, Jules Moch, André le Trocquer, and their young colleagues Pierre Bloch, Pierre Cot, Pierre Viénot, and Louis Jacquinot, held a great deal of prestige, even in the eyes of the Resistance members, for having voted, on July 10, 1940, against granting full powers to Pétain. These factors made their real influence far surpass their actual numerical percentage. By again setting up these past masters of parliamentary debate in a familiar atmosphere in Algeria, and by giving even this scant recognition to the existence of the parties, De Gaulle had put his hand in a trap. It would not let go until he had resigned from power on the morning of January 20, 1946.

On that day, De Gaulle called a meeting of his ministers* in the "war room" of the National Defense Ministry in the rue Saint-Dominique. He entered, shook hands, and, without asking the Cabinet to sit down, said: "The exclusive regime of the parties has come up again. I disapprove of it. But, unless a dictatorship is set up by force—something which I do not want and which would probably end badly—I do not have the power to stop the parties. Therefore, I must give way. On this very day, I will send the President of the National Assembly a letter informing him of the government's resignation. I sincerely thank every one of you for the help you have given me, and I ask you to remain at your posts to insure the continuity of government until your successors are appointed."

Having publicly condemned the return of the party system, and having drawn, at least for himself, the inevitable consequences, what would the General do? Would he cross the Rubicon again, or could he, on the contrary, remain on the bank while others were playing their deadly game? Could he even continue to be involved in the game, hoping all the while to dominate the other players?

This last choice was the one the General made. He declared that party politics had prevented him from running the government, yet he would attempt, on two separate occasions, to rely on a party or a pseudo-party to defend his opinions and the justice of his case. This was a great mistake, an inconsistency between his actions and his beliefs, between his tendency toward the dogmatic and his taste for the empirical. For the first time, one of the most serious symptoms of De Gaulle's ambivalence appeared. He demonstrated that split personality which, to this day, puts the results and the permanence of his work in question.

* The only members absent were Vincent Auriol and Georges Bidault, who were in London, at the first meeting of the Security Council of the U.N., and Jacques Soustelle, who was in Gabon.

DE GAULLE VANQUISHED BY THE PARTIES

On two occasions, then, De Gaulle relied on a party. The first party was the M.R.P., which, in the elections of June, 1946, received the most votes. One hundred and sixty party members were elected to Parliament. At that time, the M.R.P. was still the "party of faith" to De Gaulle. He was counting on it to carry out the program he had outlined in his speech on June 16 at Bayeux. But the M.R.P. preferred an alliance with the Socialist party to one with a man whose views seemed risky and who aroused hostile reactions in the political leaders on the left, Martinaud-Déplat and Léon Blum.

In September the break became final. De Gaulle could not rely on any existing party to fight his battles against the others—and so he founded a party of his own. This was his second great mistake. Although this party would function within the structure of the other parties, De Gaulle thought it would provide a remedy for the whole system. He thus committed the great tactical blunder of advancing into enemy territory. The man who had left French soil in order to free it now did exactly the opposite in his domestic policy.

It is true that he did not call the party he founded in April, 1947, a party. He called it a *rassemblement*—a group—the *Rassemblement du Peuple Français* (R.P.F.). Yet the R.P.F. made only one innovation. It claimed to exist outside the customary framework of political squabbles, to group Frenchmen together "above their differences of opinion." The R.P.F. welcomed members and officials of other political parties without demanding that they give up their cards. For these minor innovations to have been of any consequence, however, the R.P.F. had to distinguish itself from its adversaries by its actions. It should not have tried to reach power in the same way the other parties did.

On March 30, at Bruneval, while speaking of the formation of the new government, he specifically denounced the parties. "The day will come when the great mass of Frenchmen will reject the sterile game of party politics and reform the badly built system which destroys the nation and nullifies the state. Then they will group themselves around France."

The very next month, the great mass of Frenchmen did indeed group themselves around the *Rassemblement*. On May 1, it had 800,000 supporters, including 100,000 in Paris. Soon the R.P.F. set out on electoral campaigns, in the manner of the old parties. It made a brilliant start with the elections of October 19 and 26, 1948, when the candidates supported by the R.P.F., a movement that was only eighteen months old, won nearly 40 per cent of the votes in communities of more than 9,000 inhabitants. In Paris, they received an overwhelming majority of 52 seats, compared with 25 Communist seats, 8 Socialist, and 5 from the M.R.P.

De Gaulle then continued to play his double game, threatening to wreck the party system while actually settling into it. Right after the elections he demanded the dissolution of the National Assembly, yet within the National Assembly and the Cabinet he created a Gaullist inner group to run the Chamber of Deputies and the Senate.

From that moment, the old parties came to their senses and neutralized the intruder. Parliamentary concerns reared their head within the movement. What other party would form a coalition with them to gain a majority? Would it be the U.D.S.R., the M.R.P., the Radicals . . . ? One after the other, negotiations took place, ending in temporary compromises. Parliamentary members of the Gaullist inner group were torn between their fidelity to De Gaulle and their duty to their old party. They did not all choose the path of new loyalty: some of them actually deserted De Gaulle. Moreover, the left-wing parties were wholly committed to the Fourth Republic and were uncompromising enemies of De Gaulle.

The Radicals and the Socialists, often backed by the M.R.P., finally made a coalition to bar De Gaulle's way. On March 13, 1951, after Herriot had intervened to attack the "bigamy" of the pro-Gaullists, the Radical party censured the Gaullists within its ranks and expelled two of its white hopes, Chaban-Delmas and Michel Debré, who were out-and-out supporters of the General. Far worse, Henri Queuille, president of the Radical-Socialist party, perfected an electoral maneuver in the best tradition of backstairs politics, where, with the support of the Socialists and the M.R.P., he had a new electoral law passed which made it possible to bring the old parties into an alliance against the R.P.F. The law was the law of "pairing."

"Pairing" allowed the different parties to form a coalition in the main election, decided by a majority ballot in each department. The Seine and the Seine-et-Oise departments, however, kept the old system. To put it more precisely, when the votes were counted, the votes received by any one "paired" party could be added to those received by its "pair." If the paired parties succeeded in getting a majority, they would get all the seats, which were then divided proportionately among the winners. If they did not get a majority, the system of proportional representation would distribute the seats among all the parties, whether paired or not. This, then, was the electoral "monster" spawned by the Radicals, the S.F.I.O., and the M.R.P., the defenders of democracy, to fight the dual peril which menaced the Republic. On the left they were threatened by the red peril of the Communist party; on the right, by the Gaullist peril of the *Rassemblement du Peuple Français*. Both of these perils were, obviously, excluded from the pairing system.

It was neither more nor less than a monumental swindle, which De Gaulle was quick to denounce in public. Yet he had made this swindle possible by trying to fight on ground that the experts of the parliamentary system knew backward and forward. It was also a profitable swindle. As soon as the law was passed, R.P.F. Deputies who wanted to keep their seats saw that they faced a predictable problem of conscience—if it deserves such a term: they risked their chances of re-election. They also eliminated their hopes of becoming ministers by refusing to pair themselves with members of other parties. So the evil spell cast by the pairing system spread its web. When voting, Gaullist deputies took care not to antagonize anyone who might, when they left De Gaulle, pair with them at some future date.

On March 6, 1952, breaking with party discipline, 27 R.P.F. deputies voted for a Pinay government. Their vote gave it a majority. On June 4 the National Council of the R.P.F. passed a motion insisting on party discipline. The rebels, who refused to give in, were expelled, and the Gaullist inner group was then reduced to 89 members. De Gaulle had not intervened in the dispute. Perhaps he saw that the right time had passed, and that parliamentary tactics had contaminated even the movement he had founded to put an end to them.

On January 7, 1953, during a new ministerial crisis, no one could believe it when the entire R.P.F.—except for three members—gave its support to a government led by René Mayer, a Radical. As a result, in the elections on April 26 and May 3, the Gaullists ran into trouble.

In Paris, 10 were elected instead of 52 in 1947.

In Marseilles, 4 were elected instead of 25 in 1947.

In Lyons, 7 were elected instead of 23 in 1947.

On May 6, De Gaulle released those Gaullists who were elected. He recognized his failure: "The R.P.F.," he announced, "must steer clear of a regime which is sterile and which it cannot change for the time being. . . . The time of bankrupt illusions has come."

It was not only the bankruptcy of illusions but the bankruptcy of a political strategy based on wheeling and dealing and inferior tactics. In his retirement at Colombey, De

Gaulle was to draw his own conclusions. They were cruel, pitiless, and even cynical at times. Failures like the ones De Gaulle had just suffered harden a man. And De Gaulle was already in the habit of hiding his scruples and his weaknesses under a mask of stubbornness. He now began to wonder, with a copy of Machiavelli's *Prince* in hand, how desirable a show of frankness was in politics.

During those years of retirement, De Gaulle never ceased to voice his skepticism about the future of his country and to declare his decision never to get mixed up in its affairs. "I shall return," he announced, "if the country sends for me. I shall not play a part in any movement. I am a man alone. I belong to no one. I belong only to France."

France, unfortunately, did not seem very concerned about him. France did not react. At the beginning of May, 1958, that crucial month which would bring him to power, he again said: "France is dying. We are heading for the worst." And when Roger Frey questioned him, he said, "Nothing will happen. The country does not want to move ahead. Why should France not be pleased with Monsieur Gaillard, when Monsieur Gaillard is so pleased with himself?"

The Rubicon of Algeria

Meanwhile, the pace of events was accelerating. The Algerian War was developing into a civil war which would involve the army. De Gaulle was once again at a moment of decision. This time, however, it was a Rubicon of two streams, and De Gaulle had learned through experience to cross them one at a time.

One of the streams ran through domestic politics, which demanded reform of the government and neutralization of the party system. Backed by public opinion, De Gaulle crossed this stream easily. In 1958 he was given what Pétain had first won in July, 1940—full and immediate powers. He was also given the job of working out a new Constitution. This time, De Gaulle made no strategic errors and no blunders. He caused no confusion. He remained on his own ground, refused to put a foot in the Palais National until he was given the task of forming a government.

He was installed in office on June 1, 1958. Because of the pressure of circumstances, he took up Pétain's proposals of July, 1940. He asked for special powers, full powers, and the modification of certain articles in the Constitution. The only difference was that the opposition in Parliament was greater on July 1, 1958, than it had been on July 15, 1940. The number of Deputies who voted against him was 224, compared to 80 against Pétain. His majority was smaller too—329 instead of 569. Yet this time none of those who voted extraordinary powers to De Gaulle made themselves useless by doing away with the existing institutions of the Republic.

The second stream of the river, the Algerian problem, would be harder—it could not be bridged without bloodying the water. De Gaulle would cross it only after believing, and making others believe, that he would not cross at all.

It was a painful crossing. The consequences for a million Frenchmen were abominable. Their patriotism and courage will unfortunately go unrecognized and unrewarded. Some of the episodes of the war will stand in French history with the Saint Bartholomew and the September Massacres. Yet, even so, France simply could not maintain its political authority in Algeria. After Dienbienphu and the loss of Indochina, after England's leaving of Egypt and India, after independence in Morocco and Tunisia on Algeria's frontier, France's position there had become impossible. France could hardly be the only one with a pink spot on the map. In a changing world, Algeria would have to become independent.

It was impossible to realize how much pain this break between France and Algeria would cause. There would be inevitable hardships for a million Frenchmen. It was therefore natural that France should cling to its illusions and believe that it could keep its flag flying in North Africa. It was also natural that before the flag came down there would be desperate fighting and unforgivable revolts. It was not only Arabs who fought Frenchmen. Frenchmen fought one another.

De Gaulle was the first to sense and encourage both the illusions and the refusal to face the obvious. Before he returned to power, he categorically opposed relinquishing Algeria. On October 20, 1947, during an election campaign in Algiers, he wrote:

> We would truly become decadent if we falsely wanted to turn back the clock and lessen France's rights and duties here, or if we wanted to discourage the inhabitants of French origin who were and remain the dynamic force in Algeria, or if we wanted to encourage French Moslems to believe that separation from France would be to their advantage.

De Gaulle held these views for eleven years. Then the Algerian riots coincided curiously with Parliament's calling on De Gaulle in Paris. Thus, when he came to power again in 1958, he was asked to save French Algeria. He knew he would be.

"Never in my lifetime will the F.L.N. flag fly over Algiers," he told the military leaders in June, 1958; four years later, the F.L.N. flag was flying over Algiers. But the facts of the Algerian situation taught De Gaulle a lesson which he probably had not known before his return to power. When he realized what terrible danger France ran by continuing the war, he gradually began changing his attitude. At first he wanted to offer an honorable peace to the fellaghas. Then he wanted self-determination. Finally he admitted that Algeria would have to be Algerian, and that France would have to give it up. This solution was perhaps unavoidable, but it could have been achieved at lesser cost. De Gaulle applied Draconian measures to settle the Algerian question, using *Realpolitik* indiscriminately, for he had become the state. He allowed the ugliest and blackest tragedy in French history to take place. In the streets of Algiers the French army shot at Frenchmen who could be blamed only for wanting to remain Frenchmen.

The reason was that Algeria was a particularly painful and difficult case. Nowhere else in North Africa was there such a large population of French, or European, descent. The British would have been equally at a loss in India, had there been a similar proportion of their fellow countrymen among the Indians. France has rarely known such terrible trial in all its history.

De Gaulle found it difficult to solve the Algerian problem all at once. He knew hesitation and scruples, momentary timidity in word and deed, and this knowledge interfered with the startling boldness of his ideas and the royal integrity of his genius. People claim that the General is monolithic and set on only one course. But actually he often falters when confronted with his mission. To hide this, like so many other men in public affairs, he wears a mask. He has invented a manner for himself that makes him seem most self-confident when he feels it the least.

The way in which De Gaulle pulled France out of its worsening deadlock in domestic affairs showed this as clearly as his rise to power. But it is in his foreign policy especially that De Gaulle must be observed to be understood. The General is a man from the seventeenth century, and his motto might well be that of Descartes: *larvatus prodeo*, "Masked, I advance." One fact must be taken for granted. Since De Gaulle never moves in a straight line, one never knows what he is doing until what he is doing is finished.

CHAPTER III

De Gaulle and His Allies

MISUNDERSTANDINGS BETWEEN ALLIES

In time of war and crisis, the relationship between allies might be thought to be one of mutual understanding, trust, and co-operation. Not so where De Gaulle and his allies are concerned. In no other relations does the General arouse more misunderstanding and surprise, repeatedly disappointing those who admire him and would like to count on him.

At the beginning of June, 1964, I found myself in New York during the celebration of the twentieth anniversary of the landings in Normandy. De Gaulle's refusal to attend the ceremonies caused a great stir in the American press. A few specialists on European politics, among them Walter Lippmann, analyzed the reasons for this refusal and were not too offended, but most Americans were scandalized. I was forced to answer a barrage of questions in radio and television interviews, all of which showed up the dismay of my interviewers. "What difference is there between De Gaulle and Napoleon?" "Is it true that De Gaulle still bases his actions on the grudges he felt against Roosevelt twenty years ago?" "Is it true that he works hand in glove with the Communists?" "How do you explain it?" "Why does he hate us? And does he hate the English?" "What can we do to understand him, and to make him understand us?"

These questions may seem excessive, but they are far from pointless. They showed, however, a misunderstanding of

France only equalled by French misunderstanding of American politics.

What was even more extraordinary was the atmosphere of those interviews. Under the sting of De Gaulle's refusal, which was taken as an insult, all the deep, complex, and permanent feelings of Americans toward France rose to the surface: their tremendous sympathy and affection for France, their fondness for its culture and its language (for years, French has been the main foreign language taught at the university and high school levels, though the French-speaking ethnic group is not nearly so large as the German, Spanish, or Italian). To be French in New York is the best recommendation one can have; no other nationality arouses so much spontaneous and active good will. But it is an exacting friendship. America does not allow its friends to get away with anything, and it naturally expects something in return for its help.

America does not always get it, and because of De Gaulle, it seems in fact to get back nothing but ingratitude. The Americans justly feel that they liberated the French in 1944; they also feel that they helped France to conquer starvation and slump after the war, and that they defended France against Communist pressure. Why, therefore, after its complete recovery, does France treat them so badly?

In reality all these grudges held by America against France and by France against America simply demonstrate two things. First, they show that the Americans, after helping a nation in distress, now feel rather disappointed that they can no longer be charitable toward the French. This often happens. "France is doing well, too well," the Americans think. "Let's hope that she won't begin to annoy her neighbors again and flex her muscles too soon." Second, the grudges show that De Gaulle raises problems which the Americans cannot solve, but they confuse these problems with "the French problem."

It is true that De Gaulle treats the Americans roughly; but no one understands why. The Americans have the tremendous quality of always being ready to consider new ideas; they are always eager to learn what they do not know. So they tell themselves that De Gaulle must have reasons for his behavior —but he is wrong not to give them. His pride is hard to swallow, his disdain intolerable. But after all, this maddening man has accomplished some rather difficult things in his lifetime. So Americans, who have a sense of fair play and who like efficiency, who excuse almost anything "if it works," end up by asking themselves if De Gaulle's arrogance does not hide something else. They quite naturally wonder if there is not something good and useful to be learned from De Gaulle's knowledge of the world and his gift of prophecy.

It is important to realize that De Gaulle disturbs America as he disturbs France. Both countries would like him to be less brutal; would like to pay a cheaper price, in body and soul, for the new truths that he gives to the world. But people are beginning to understand that, though his balance sheet is often slow and clumsy and painful to read, and the debit column is long, De Gaulle is one of the men of today whose credits are totally beyond the conventional and everyday.

He also disturbs England, which probably has a slightly uneasy conscience about De Gaulle. If the United States has opposed the General, it has done so openly, without concealing its intentions. In the beginning, the English did everything in their power to help De Gaulle; he would have gotten nowhere without them. Right to the end, British military and political aid was one of the main factors in the French comeback. Yet the Intelligence Service, a secret branch of the English diplomatic service which stayed in the shadow of alliances or treaties of friendship, often gave the lie to the treaties between De Gaulle and Britain and interpreted the agreements to suit itself. By hidden ruses and apparent frankness it made sure that Britain would get the lion's share of anything at the expense of its partners. The lion was also a fox. De Gaulle got a hint of this, especially in the Levant. As much as every individual Englishman showed loyalty, friendship, and tact toward the Frenchmen who were regrouping on his soil to carry on the fight after the fall of France, that much the Secret Service, and sometimes other services, took advantage of the occasion to nibble away at France's political and economic position in key areas of the globe. In his *Memoirs*,* De Gaulle gave a masterly description of the workings of the "British Machine." Its wheels were sometimes visible, but its gears were hidden. "The concentrated efforts, the endless means, the insistence—sometimes gracious, sometimes pressing or menacing—that the English were capable of using to get what they wanted had to be lived through to be imagined." At the head of it sat the living symbol of the double game, Winston Churchill. That great friend of France, that dangerous partner, was both sincere and sly, disinterested and shrewd.

The Americans can justifiably feel surprised by De Gaulle's brutality toward them, but the English, frankly, have not a reason in the world to be outraged. The only thing they can sincerely hold against him is that he did not give in to them when so many statesmen, French and others, would have been only too delighted to do so.

Perhaps another minor grievance is De Gaulle's overly regal manner, which outrages the old monarchy of Britain. One day, with some English friends, I was watching De Gaulle speak on television. As usual he used the third person when talking about himself. "What do you think of him?" I asked, when the speech was over. There was a silence. "We think that, in England, not even the Queen would express herself in that way."

* *The Complete War Memoirs of Charles de Gaulle* (New York: Simon and Schuster, 1959).

The Anglo-Saxon countries are not the only ones to feel disturbed by De Gaulle. He worries the Dutch, the Belgians, the Germans; the Russians and Chinese, who sense that his advances are not disinterested and that they ought to be wary of his long-term views; the new nations of North Africa and Black Africa, the two Vietnams. He towers above other contemporary statesmen and breeds more misunderstandings, both favorable and unfavorable, then any other man. The existence of these misunderstandings should not be camouflaged or denied, as some of De Gaulle's apologists have done.

DIFFERENT CLASSES OF ALLIES

During his career, De Gaulle has had two kinds of allies, first-class and second-class. His first-class allies are the ones who are permanently and genuinely allies, whose civilizations have strong ties with France's, whose future goals are the same as the General's. De Gaulle handles these allies roughly, uncompromisingly, and often brutally, because he is sure that a feeling of kinship will survive all squabbles and storms. These are De Gaulle's "super-allies," mainly the Anglo-Saxon countries, Great Britain and the United States.

After these come his more transient or doubtful allies. De Gaulle knows that he has nothing in common with their regimes, their ideologies, their philosophies, or their faiths; they are his allies only according to their momentary situation on the political chessboard, on which he has to play, but to whom he never commits himself for good. Among these second-class allies, these "enemy-allies," are China and the U.S.S.R. He treats them in the opposite way from his "super-allies," cloaking his criticisms and refusals in amiability and approaches; he is not well disposed toward them, he just puts on a smiling mask while he prepares a snare for them and maneuvers to make use of them.

DE GAULLE AND GREAT BRITAIN

De Gaulle has always been stubborn with his first-class allies. In the beginning, Britain was his one ally, until the Wehrmacht began the attack on Russia on June 22, 1941, so that during his first year as a rebel De Gaulle depended solely and entirely on England and had no chance to maneuver or switch.

Yet within the first few days of his coming to power in critical circumstances, he showed that he had a mind of his own. He later justified himself in the noblest terms: "Since I was reduced to a few rags and tatters of strength and national pride, I had to answer, all alone, for the fate of a nation that had been delivered into the hands of the enemy and torn asunder."

Only three weeks after his arrival in London and his first appeal on the B.B.C., De Gaulle made the fact clear that he did not intend to become the puppet of the English; he planned to keep his freedom of speech and his liberty of action. On July 8, 1940, he was still like a bird in the wilderness. There had been no agreement with Winston Churchill to assure his status or that of his volunteers. All Churchill had to do to stop De Gaulle from speaking over the radio was to lift a finger. And yet, on that day, the British Prime Minister was rebuked over the B.B.C. by the General, who spoke as if he were already installed in Paris and represented his entire country.

The issue was, indeed, an important one. A horrible incident had taken place. The British had sunk the French navy off Mers-el-Kebir, for despite all the assurances and promises of the Vichy government and the French admirals, both written and oral, Winston Churchill was afraid that the French navy would be handed over to Germany. On July 2,

1940, he sent an order to Admiral Somerville, commander of the H Force of the Royal Navy, to carry out what he called "one of the most disagreeable and difficult missions ever to be undertaken by a British admiral." "And one of the most dishonorable," he might have added. For Somerville had to attack the French fleet, anchored at Mers-el-Kebir, near Oran, without any warning except a last-minute ultimatum. Because of the clauses of the armistice with Germany, the French fleet was in no position to fight. The ultimatum was not accepted, and before the French ships could prepare for battle, they were sunk at close range by British gunfire. The English ships could act without fear of counterattack, for they were out at sea, and they fired over a rocky point which protected them. It was a massacre without glory. Over the B.B.C. on July 8, De Gaulle described the event in the following terms:

First, I want to say this: there is not a single Frenchman who heard of the sinking of the French fleet by our Allies without feeling a grief and rage which come from his innermost self. There is no reason why we should suppress this feeling, and I mean to express it openly. So I turn to the English, asking them to spare us and to spare themselves from claiming that this odious tragedy was a real naval victory. This claim would be unjust and out of place.

The ships at Oran were actually in no state to fight. They were docked and they had no opportunity to maneuver or disperse. They were manned by officers and crews who had lived through a great moral crisis during the past two weeks. They allowed the English ships to fire first, and as everyone knows, that is decisive at sea and at such distances. Their destruction was not the result of a glorious battle. A French soldier declares this to his British allies all the more sharply because he holds their navy in high esteem.

Nonetheless, once he had spoken out, De Gaulle justified Churchill's action. With knowing it was false, he claimed that "due to a dishonorable agreement, the former government in Bordeaux had agreed to surrender our ships at the discretion of the enemy." Even so, considering the time and the circumstances, De Gaulle had demonstrated his independence from those who supported him.

This first skirmish was fought with blunted swords. A second would influence the whole course of the relationship between De Gaulle and Churchill. On August 7, 1940, an agreement was signed by the two men who were committed to the war against Germany. Churchill, of course, had at his disposal the untapped resources of a vast empire, whereas De Gaulle had only the backing of a few men who had escaped from almost total disaster. Yet besides the material and financial support which he needed, De Gaulle also won his principal demands in this document: he was recognized as the leader of all the Free French, obtaining the pledge that "His Majesty's Government is resolved to guarantee the complete restoration of French greatness and independence, once the Allied armies are victorious." It was also finally agreed that the French troops recruited by General de Gaulle "will never have to bear arms against France."

Judging by the text, De Gaulle should have been completely satisfied; he had won every guarantee for the future. In fact, his victory was neither so simple nor so absolute, for Churchill had written a secret letter which narrowly defined the terms of agreement and sent this to De Gaulle as the official agreement was being published and broadcast all over the world to prove that France would remain permanently in the Allied camp. In this secret letter Churchill specified that the expression "the complete restoration of French greatness and independence" did not necessarily involve territorial frontiers. In other words, France might still have to cede some areas.

Churchill also explained that the expression "will never have to bear arms against France" had to be interpreted as meaning a France that was free to choose its own course and was not directly or indirectly under the pressure of the Germans. The clause did not cover the troops that had remained loyal to the Vichy government. In other words, a fratricidal battle between Gaullist and Vichyite soldiers was still a possibility. De Gaulle had to concede these points, but he hoped that circumstances would "one day allow the British government to view these questions with fewer reservations."

Thus, from the very beginning of his relationship with Churchill, De Gaulle could see that their points of view did not necessarily coincide. England would back him only in its own interests; he had to tread cautiously. The future was to prove him right. On September 21, 1940, hardly three months after his formal recognition over the B.B.C., De Gaulle learned that the British government had sent General Catroux to Egypt without his consent. He considered the choice of Catroux completely justifiable, but since he had not been the one to make the decision, he decided to oppose it. He complained to the Prime Minister about this violation of their agreement, to which Churchill immediately replied by telegram, giving in. It was "perfectly understood that [Catroux] holds his appointment from you only, and I shall again make this clear to him."

And so De Gaulle always had to be on the alert. In the whole course of his relationship with England, he stayed either on the defensive or the offensive, sometimes counter-attacking in a way that was brutal or unexpected. Yet the reason for this was that all British Prime Ministers, from Winston Churchill to Macmillan, behaved in the same way—a way that never varied over the years, whatever the circumstances.

On December 16, 1941, Churchill proposed a war strategy to Roosevelt in which he shamelessly asked for a "revision," that is, a betrayal of his agreement with De Gaulle. "The time has come," he wrote,

to give Vichy and North Africa the choice between a blessing and a curse. The blessing would be an agreement guaranteed by the United States and Great Britain, by which France would regain its status as a great power and all of its territories. . . . [As we have seen, Churchill had refused to make a similar agreement with De Gaulle.] Our relations with General de Gaulle and the Free French movement will have to be revised. Until now, the United States has not committed itself as I have in my correspondence with the general. . . . If Vichy were disposed to act as we desire over North Africa, the United States and Great Britain would have to work at a reconciliation between the Free French [the Gaullists] and the other Frenchmen who would again take up arms against Germany. Inversely, if Vichy persists in its collaboration with the Germans, and if we are obliged to make a forced landing in North and West Africa, we would then have to support and use to the full the Gaullist movement.*

Nothing could have been more Machiavellian. But, in Churchill's case, there was at least one compensation. When he played the double game, he did it openly and deliberately, sometimes even indulging in the luxury of warning his rival. On August 7, 1942, at lunch with De Gaulle in Cairo, he said, "I am about to reorganize our High Command. At the same time, I will see what is the state of our quarrel with you over Syria. Then I shall go to Moscow. That will give you an idea of how important my journey is. I have been a little worried." "It is true that those three questions are vital," De Gaulle replied. "The first one is entirely your own concern. The second one concerns me, and the third one concerns Stalin mainly. You will have to tell him that the Second Front will not be opened this year, so I understand your anxiety. But you will manage easily, as long as your conscience is clear." "I would like you to know that my conscience is an easygoing sort of girl. I can always fix her," Churchill grumbled.

De Gaulle would often remember the remark in the long course of his dealings with Churchill, and with England. He must, indeed, have remembered it during the days before the

* Paul-Marie de la Gorce, *De Gaulle entre Deux Mondes* (Paris: Librairie Arthème Fayard, 1964).

Allied landing in France on June 6, 1944. During that period, for security reasons, the British authorities in Algiers prevented him from getting in touch with both his military representative in London, General Koenig, and his Ambassador, Viénot. De Gaulle was so furious and suspicious that, without further ado, he broke off relations with his British allies. Only after the King saw Koenig and allowed him to send a cable to De Gaulle in Algiers, after the English press openly deplored the incident and showed great understanding toward De Gaulle, and finally Eden, in the House of Commons, and Churchill himself spoke out, was the situation smoothed over.

All this show of regret bore some fruit. Churchill sent a private plane for De Gaulle so that he could be in England on the day of the landing. De Gaulle seemed reluctant, for no one had consulted or even warned him about the landing. But finally he pretended to give in to the pressure of his ministers and climbed into the airplane. He even accepted an invitation to lunch with Churchill on June 4; it would be an excellent opportunity for him to tell the Prime Minister what he thought. But he would do no more, and would refuse everything that Churchill asked of him. He refused to place the French liaison officers at the disposal of the Allied troops, although he had trained these officers in Algiers especially for that purpose; he refused to participate in radio broadcasts to the French population, although other heads of state, leaders of governments in exile in London, and even Eisenhower, spoke. During the night of June 5, while the first troops were preparing to land on French shores, Churchill asked the French Ambassador, Viénot, to come to see him. He persuaded Viénot to try one last appeal to De Gaulle that night, to get De Gaulle to soften his attitude because of the circumstances. The next morning, Viénot described his attempt to the English Prime Minister: "I have never been so bawled out in all my life, Mr. Prime Minister."

At the very time that Allied unity was more imperative than ever, De Gaulle was at his most impossible. His behavior was shocking, yet it might be justified by later evidence of Allied plans for the future of the General and of France. Putting aside the American records for the moment and concentrating on the English ones, a vindication for De Gaulle's suspicions begins to emerge. On May 13, 1943, Churchill had said to the American Secretary of State, Cordell Hull, that both he and Eden "found De Gaulle impossible," and that personally, Churchill was "completely disgusted by De Gaulle." On June 4, 1944, almost on the eve of the landing in Normandy, Churchill announced De Gaulle's arrival to Roosevelt in terms that leave little doubt as to his real feelings:

"A large majority of the *Comité de Gaulle* has decided that the general had to accept my invitation to come here. He muttered and grumbled; but Massigli and various others threatened to resign if he refused. We are waiting for him on D — 1. If he comes, Eisenhower will see him for half an hour to explain the situation to him from the purely military point of view. I shall go back to London during the night of D-day. I don't expect we will be able to do much with De Gaulle."*

This English reserve was not merely verbal, nor was it just a matter of the moment, the result of exceptional circumstances, such as the landings in France. During the whole of his relationship with England, De Gaulle had sensed this reserve, and felt the unofficial attitude behind the official one. Sometimes this had led to bursts of temper and serious quarrels. In April and May of 1945, for example, the English supported underground activities against France in Libya and Syria, two countries then under French mandate. De Gaulle reacted by using all the diplomatic resources at his disposal and by sending in troops to restore peace in both countries, which they succeeded in doing without bloodshed. This was

* Winston Churchill, *The Second World War* (Boston: Houghton Mifflin, 1953).

not what Churchill had wanted; he wanted to humiliate France and then to take its place in Libya and Syria. Once the fighting was over, he presented De Gaulle with an ultimatum, which he had first submitted to Parliament though this was not customary. "In order to avoid any collision between the British and the French forces [the fighting was already over], we request that you [De Gaulle] give the French troops immediate orders to cease fire and to retire to their quarters." The text was devious: Churchill wanted France to lose face by seeming to back down under a British ultimatum, though it was merely carrying out what it already intended to do. And so, on June 4, 1945, De Gaulle summoned the English Ambassador in Paris. "I acknowledge the fact that we are not in a position to go to war with you at the present time. But you have insulted France and betrayed the West. This cannot be forgotten." And De Gaulle never forgot. His recent decisions regarding the United Kingdom perhaps have their origin in his threat of twenty years' standing.

Is De Gaulle right to hold a grudge against Britain? Is he not being petty to let himself be influenced, twenty years after the event, by the memory of an insult that happened in entirely different circumstances? Or is there wisdom in this course after all, a wisdom gained by long experience? De Gaulle is certainly not completely anti-British. His harshness to Churchill is tempered by a certain esteem, an attitude which was wholly reciprocated. "I agree with you," Churchill wrote to President Roosevelt on June 18, 1943. "It is impossible to trust De Gaulle's friendship for the Allies. But many members of my Cabinet, myself included, cannot forget that he joined us during the darkest hours, and that he tried to carry on the struggle against the Germans. The man is impossible, but one must take those facts into account."

De Gaulle also took into account some facts that made him appreciate his war partner.

It is true that Churchill did not spare me when I was his ally. His behavior over the subject of the Levant was, at worst, even that of an enemy. All in all, he supported me as long as I was the leader of a French faction which favored him and which he could use. . . . But when he saw me represent an ambitious France, which seemed to want to recover its power in Europe and overseas, he felt within him the breath of Pitt himself. In spite of everything, one essential, unforgettable fact remained: without him, my effort would have been useless from the very start. By then lending me a strong and helping hand, he essentially aided France.*

This said, De Gaulle's reasons for being suspicious of the English—and his reasons for acting on those suspicions—must not be underestimated. His grudges, if they still exist, would not explain why he still distrusts Britain and why his reserve toward the English endures. If he still bears a grudge against England and always will, it is because he realized, in his dealings with the English, that they, too, have one permanent trait: they are Machiavellis, cloaked in courtesy and decked out with friendliness, and he is sure that the inner feelings and the outer behavior of the English will never alter. Macmillan's attitude certainly did nothing to remove the General's prejudices. For in December, 1962, the English Prime Minister unexpectedly switched course. In the space of a few days he deserted Europe, over the Skybolt affair, and drew closer to America.

If the British do not change, why should De Gaulle? "Let the English shoot first," he might say, paraphrasing a famous quotation. De Gaulle's attitude toward Great Britain is logical and coherent. It is based on personal experience and firsthand analysis. Is the same true of De Gaulle's policy toward the United States?

DE GAULLE AND THE UNITED STATES

England was De Gaulle's only ally from June 18, 1940, until June 22, 1941. It was a first-class ally, with the same goal and much the same culture as France.

* *The Complete War Memoirs*, Vol. III.

On June 22, a new ally was forced, by aggression and in spite of itself, to join the original Allies. This was the U.S.S.R., a dictatorship and a second-class ally. Although the Russian government was totalitarian, and although he opposed Communism, Churchill immediately pledged his support to Russia. De Gaulle, who was in the Levant, took the same position. Two days after the German attack he telegraphed his London offices: "Without any discussion, for the time being, of the vices and even the crimes of the Soviet regime, we must proclaim, as Churchill has done, that we are fully committed to the Russians, because they are fighting the Germans . . . the airplanes, the tanks, and the German soldiers that the Russians destroy will no longer be there to prevent us from liberating France." In this fashion, De Gaulle gave a precise definition of the country that was, and has remained for him, a second-class ally. He asked Professor René Cassin to meet the Russian Ambassador to Great Britain. On August 12, Cassin asked if Russia, following England's example, planned to make a public declaration of its intention to restore France's independence and greatness. Maisky answered that it would. De Gaulle also wanted to know if, by any chance, Russia would guarantee France's territorial possessions. To this question, no answer was given. France's dealings with Moscow brought no particular problems until 1944.

At the end of 1941, on December 7, a new first-class ally, the United States, appeared on the scene, also because of an unexpected act of aggression. Russia might never have gone over to the Allied camp had it not been for a decision by Hitler, but in the case of the United States, the Japanese attack on Pearl Harbor merely hastened its inevitable decision to enter the war on the side of England. The difference between the first-class ally and the second-class ally was clear in the very way they entered the war.

De Gaulle's reaction to his newest ally was, apparently, as paradoxical, unexpected, and improper as could be imagined.

Only eleven days after Pearl Harbor, despite the assurances of Admiral Muselier and the formal disapproval of the American government, De Gaulle decided to seize the archipelago of Saint Pierre and Miquelon, *manu militari*. These two islands near Newfoundland had previously been under the control of Vichy. During the night of December 24, the only policeman on duty at the port of Saint Pierre was unable to halt a landing force which outnumbered him by at least three hundred to one. De Gaulle's excuse was one used by all heads of state in similar situations to justify an arbitrary decision: one does something to prevent someone else from doing it. Churchill justified his questionable attack on the French fleet at Mers-el-Kebir by claiming that the ships of his ex-ally were about to join the enemy; Hitler attacked Russia pretending that Russia was about to attack Germany; Roosevelt was to land his troops in North Africa, claiming that Axis troops were ready to land. In the case of the archipelago, De Gaulle justified his snub of the United States by saying that the Canadian government meant to land there and destroy Saint Pierre's radio station.

There were two real reasons for taking over the islands. One was that De Gaulle would have the chance of winning a referendum in his favor from a population of French origin. In this way he would set a precedent, in the eyes of world opinion, for the referendum he would use in the future to confirm his legitimacy.

The second reason was to give a very severe warning to the United States. The Americans had persisted, ever since the Armistice, in considering the Vichy government a legitimate one. They ignored the *Comité de Gaulle*, and had an annoying habit of always backing the wrong French leaders.

At first the Americans had backed General Fornel de la Laurencie, whom they considered head of the Resistance in France in 1941, although he was far better known in Vichy, as the Marshal's representative in the Occupied Zone, than in any *maquis*. It was De la Laurencie who believed that he was showing great political acumen when in reply to the question, "What will you do with De Gaulle?" he answered succinctly, "De Gaulle? We shall pardon him." In 1942 the Americans had backed Weygand, had wanted to make him the head of North Africa, which they were preparing to liberate, but Weygand had declared that he was "too old to be a rebel." In 1943 they backed Giraud, who agreed to lead the French troops in North Africa against the Axis powers, and after Darlan's death Giraud also led the government in North Africa, thus drawing De Gaulle's fire on two counts. Less than a year later, this would lead to Giraud's downfall.

There was only one man whom the Americans obstinately refused to back as leader of the Resistance or chief of the rebels, and this was the man who would win. For two years De Gaulle had been demonstrating his talent as political agitator and military organizer, yet the Americans were just as reluctant as at the beginning to recognize him as the head of the French government. As far as they were concerned, there was only one legitimate leader of France, and that was Pétain. This attitude was not unreasonable at the beginning of the war, but it would become so before the United States realized it. In July, 1944, the U.S. was still backing a last-minute effort to keep both Pétain and Laval afloat. De Gaulle may have become convinced that in European and, in particular, French matters, the United States was not so well informed or clearsighted as it should be.

Admiral Leahy was the great supporter of this policy in the White House. Leahy, who had been United States Ambassador to Vichy until diplomatic relations were broken off in November, 1942, was a perfectly honorable man, of unquestionable integrity, but was he really qualified to represent his country in an abnormal situation during a time of upheaval? And could a country which sent such men as representatives be serious in its attitudes toward France? Leahy was rather like Trinity Church, at the end of Wall Street in New York City, dwarfed by skyscrapers and surrounded by banks. He too was dwarfed by the circumstances in which he had to carry out his mission; dwarfed by the gigantic forces that bore down, either directly or indirectly, on Pétain's government, encircling it, neutralizing it, then finally annihilating it completely. He was an old-fashioned American, the relic of an age when the mercantile circles of New England still made up the elite of the American population. And Pétain was another relic of a bygone age, that of the First World War. The two old men sympathized with and understood each other, but when they met in Vichy all they seemed to understand was each other. And so, both at Vichy and after his return to Washington, Leahy in perfectly good faith influenced President Roosevelt in the direction of his own prejudices.

One unpublished detail is evidence of this: when De Gaulle went to New York and Washington in July, 1944, he organized a reception whose invitation cards displeased Admiral Leahy. In his memoirs,* Leahy criticizes the wording of these invitations, which, according to him, read:

> *"General de Gaulle,*
> *Of the Provisional Government of the French Republic,*
> *requests the pleasure of your company. . . ."*

Leahy wrote, "This was generally accepted as a public announcement of his self-assumed position as Provisional President of the French Republic."

Those who got this impression were probably touchy and rather hostile. The fact that De Gaulle mentioned his membership in the G.P.R.F. on the invitations without mentioning that he led it does not prove he should not have done so. Yet, when diplomatic subtleties are in question, a man cannot be too cautious.

It turns out, however, that De Gaulle was not as diplomatic

---

* *I Was There* (New York: McGraw-Hill, 1950).

as all that, and that Admiral Leahy's account is at fault. Ambassador Brasseur, a French diplomat who was in New York in 1944 and a Gaullist representative, recently showed me one of these famous invitations. I saw with my own eyes how it was worded:

"General de Gaulle,
<u>President</u> *of the Provisional Government of the French Republic,*
requests the pleasure of your company. . . ."

As often happens to lesser men than diplomats and admirals, Leahy had made a mistake. He had probably altered his account to suit his own and his government's prejudices. This is a limited but positive proof of the way in which Washington tended to view De Gaulle while Roosevelt was President.

There is a great difference between the attitude of the United States and that of England toward De Gaulle. In the case of the United States, there is no Machiavellianism. Perhaps American policy could rather be called too unsubtle and too naïve. The Foreign Office is dangerous because it knows too much; the White House could be dangerous because it knows too little.

DE GAULLE AND THE WHITE HOUSE

Every time the occupant of the White House changes, De Gaulle, if he is in power, has to feel his way and size up the newcomer. He has done this with Roosevelt, Truman, Eisenhower, and Kennedy in turn. Has he yet decided about President Johnson?

On the whole, Roosevelt did not like De Gaulle. France's weakened position suited him perfectly. For both these reasons his dealings with the General were frequently not very friendly or very frank. On June 17, 1943, fifteen days after De Gaulle arrived in Algiers to share power provisionally with

Giraud, Roosevelt wrote to Churchill: "I am fed up with de Gaulle. . . . I am absolutely convinced that he has jeopardized, and continues to jeopardize, our war effort, and that he represents a great threat to us. He likes neither the English nor the Americans. . . . I agree with you that the time has come for us to part company with him." In spite of many attempts, the time never came.

Even more characteristic of Roosevelt's feeling toward De Gaulle and France is a memorandum from him to Winston Churchill, dated May 8, 1943.

I am terribly sorry, but it seems to me that the bride [de Gaulle] is becoming more and more unbearable. The war in North Africa [the Tunisian campaign] has almost reached its objective, without any material contribution from de Gaulle. In civilian matters the situation seems, for all its dangers, to be on the right track. Yet, there can be no doubt that de Gaulle is setting his vicious staff of propagandists to work in Algiers. Their job is to sow discord among the various elements of the population, particularly the Arabs and the Jews. He is in the process of expanding the strength of his group of agitators. They spend their time setting up counter-demonstrations and even riots. Unfortunately, there are already too many who are beginning to believe that these disorders are partly or wholly financed by funds from the British government. . . .

De Gaulle may be a good man. But he has a messianic complex. Furthermore, he is convinced that the French people support him personally. I doubt it. I believe that the French people support the Free French movement, and that it doesn't know who de Gaulle is, and that its heart goes out to the noble aims that the movement had when it was started. . . .

If the French people only knew what you and I know about de Gaulle, they would continue to support the movement, but not the man who is its present leader in London. This is why I am more and more concerned about de Gaulle's continuous machinations. . . .

The paragraphs which follow contained two definite threats to France's independence, and, as a chain reaction, to the happiness of a French overseas territory, the large island of Madagascar:

I tend to think that when we go into France, we will have to think of a military occupation, with British and American generals in charge. I think that this might prove to be necessary for six months, or even a year, after our coming to France. This will give the French the time they need to prepare for elections and to form a new government. . . .

I think we could eventually consider the creation of an entirely new French committee, whose members could not be appointed without your approval and mine. Giraud should be named Commander in Chief of the French nation and of the army. . . . I don't know what to do about de Gaulle. Perhaps you could appoint him Governor of Madagascar.

The inhabitants of Madagascar had a narrow escape. And yet, one part of these unexpected and rather unrealistic plans was almost carried out. Liberated France came within a hairsbreadth of being administered by the Allied leaders. An "Amgot" (Allied Military Government of Occupied Territories) like the one in Italy was almost set up. Even certain preliminary steps were taken, such as the printing of banknotes for France, stamped "made in U.S.A."* But De Gaulle's stubborn resistance forced the Americans to review their policy. De Gaulle was received by Roosevelt in Washington on July 2, 1944, and it was only after that interview that the American President recognized De Gaulle's government.

Apparently the two men ended up by liking each other a great deal. De Gaulle surpassed himself in a show of democratic simplicity; Roosevelt surpassed himself with a show of

* Robert Aron, *France Reborn: The History of the Liberation* (New York: Scribner, 1964).

aristocratic charm. Each man wore the mask which his opponent wanted to see, but neither was taken in. When De Gaulle left Washington, he knew that he had won a battle but not the war. With someone like Roosevelt, the game would have to be played over and over again. Roosevelt sent De Gaulle a photograph of himself inscribed: "To General de Gaulle, who is my friend," which did not prevent him from writing to Churchill, "I believe that he [de Gaulle] is basically an egotist." Once the official warmth of the reception was over, the two men became as reticent as before. Roosevelt remained mistrustful, De Gaulle skeptical about the good will lavished on him. The atmosphere soon became charged with misunderstanding again.

On Fedruary 12, 1945, after the conference at Yalta, to which he was not invited, De Gaulle received a letter from Roosevelt which he judged "untimely." The American President informed De Gaulle that he wanted to meet with the French leader, and he himself fixed the place—on French territory, in Algiers—and reserved the right to choose the date as well. De Gaulle's reaction was firm. On the very next day, he states in his *Memoirs*,* he wrote the United States Ambassador, Jefferson Caffery,

that it was impossible for me to go to Algiers at the present time, without warning, and that for this reason I very much regretted the fact that I would not be able to receive President Roosevelt there; that the French government had invited him to come to Paris in November, and had very much regretted that he had not been able to come then; but that we would be very happy to welcome him in the capital, if he wished to come at any time; and that if he wished, during his trip, to stop in Algiers all the same, I hoped he would be kind enough to warn us, so that we could give the Governor General the necessary instructions to do everything to meet his wishes.

* *The Complete War Memoirs.*

Roosevelt was dying when he received this reply. De Gaulle was unaware that he was starting a controversy with a man on the threshold of eternity, and had he known it, would he have taken it into account? Two months later, on April 12, Truman took Roosevelt's place. De Gaulle was satisfied with the change. Truman seemed to him less complicated, more direct, more practical than Roosevelt had been. "When he spoke, one felt far removed from the vastly idealistic schemes that used to pour forth in the office of his illustrious predecessor." Less utopian than Roosevelt and also less devious, the new occupant of the White House had "given up the plan for world harmony, and had admitted that the competition between the Free World and the Soviet World would henceforth dominate everything." In this respect, Truman took up views that De Gaulle had been expressing for a long time.

But though the problem had been correctly stated, Truman's solutions seemed a bit too simplified, a bit too Yankee, for the General. According to Truman, America was the great model which the whole world, regardless of its diversity and its problems, ought to copy. As De Gaulle said, not without irony, "For a people to be perfect, all it has to do is to practice democracy in the same way as the New World." The American states, which shared the same origins and language, succeeded only after a bloody Civil War in getting along together and prospering in a federal union. Truman wanted to know why France and Germany, who had clashed as violently as the Northerners and the Southerners, could not get together in a federal union. In 1945 this prospect made De Gaulle smile. Yet fifteen years later he would come round to it himself. He let Truman talk on and then expounded his own, very different, solution to the German problem: an end to a centralized Reich, a self-governing state on the left bank of the Rhine, and an international regime in the Ruhr.

In this case, the American President anticipated the solutions of the future much more accurately than De Gaulle.

The General was rather like Christopher Columbus, who discovered America trying to find a route to India: De Gaulle did not then foresee the policies he would adopt. His attitude toward Germany then was the attitude of France after the First World War—one of revenge and reparations—a factor that had led to the Second World War. Nothing in De Gaulle's thinking indicated his amazing change of mind in the future.

De Gaulle smiled, perhaps with good reason, when Truman explained that the free enterprise system was a universal cure-all; it would guarantee world peace and prosperity. The possibility that the world, or part of it, would reject capitalism seemed preposterous at the time. It would take another fifteen years for this possibility to become the totally expected. For as Henry IV's good French minister, Sully, would have put it, America had two breasts in 1945. Both were mechanized. From one came gold, from the other fire. America had a monopoly on dollars and atomic bombs; it had nothing to fear in the world. And so a skeptical De Gaulle had to yield before these ideas of global politics. For him they represented only a transient and fragile moment in history. They did not bother him.

What was really important was to get dollars without asking for them. In an Old World style reminiscent of Louis XIV he said, "We took advantage of the occasion of my trip to Washington to conclude the negotiations undertaken for many months by Jean Monnet. They involved 650 million dollars that America was lending us on a long-term loan, at a time when it was putting an end to Lend-Lease."* What mattered even more was that France, which was having a hard time re-establishing itself as a world power, should not be thwarted and threatened by American "leadership." On this point Truman gave all the assurances he could. In other words, he did not mention the aid that he was giving England to carry on policies that hardly favored French interests.

* *Ibid.,* Vol. III.

Where he was not committed to England, the American President promised whatever the General wanted. But the best head of state in the world can give only what he has, or at least what he has left. And so he guaranteed France that the United States would not pick a quarrel with France over Indochina. He also guaranteed that a Franco-Anglo-American committee would immediately be set up in the Ruhr. De Gaulle's mocking smile took on a hint of contentment. Of course America was following a different policy from his, and of course there could be no question of "understanding or unlimited trust." But the General could see Truman's "frankness," and he found it an improvement over Roosevelt's attitude. He took away with him "the impression of a head of state well adapted to his post, with a practical turn of mind that led to practical policies; in other words, a man who doubtless did not expect any miracles, but who could certainly be counted on in an emergency."

In fact, during the whole time that Truman was in the White House, De Gaulle refrained from those sudden, often tempestuous displays of pride and righteousness for which he has become known.

Eisenhower was a military colleague, a general, and a victorious general at that. These credentials gave De Gaulle every reason to respect Eisenhower, but since he distrusts other soldiers, they gave him a few reasons to suspect him as well. When Eisenhower came to Paris on September 2, 1959, De Gaulle spoke of his friendly feelings which had grown during the fight for freedom:

"It is with deep joy that I find again in President Eisenhower that dear, good, loyal companion with whom I proceeded down a very hard stage on the road of history."

Unfortunately, 1959 was different from 1944; history now parted the two men. For Eisenhower, history meant following in Truman's footsteps, but even more in Roosevelt's. He had to confirm America's leadership of the world. He therefore had to consolidate the political and military foundations of American power, the United Nations, and especially NATO, where the armed forces of various European powers were integrated under one command, usually American.

When De Gaulle returned to power in 1958, French policy changed from a European one, a part of a Western system led by America. Either France was to have, along with the Americans and the English, a major voice, a special responsibility, and an exceptional role in leading the West, or it would withdraw from NATO, remove its troops from the common organization, and take over responsibility for the essential part of its own defense by creating its own atomic force—revival of a worn-out nationalism, in an age when everyone was thinking in terms of a federal Europe. In spite of De Gaulle, a federal Europe is probably the solution of the future best suited to the Christian civilization of the West. But, according to him, so far this plan has too often been a cover for non-European interests. And this is the essential point: he feels that its aim is to allow the United States to continue to dominate the world, if need be at the expense of the smaller nations or against their national interests. It was on this point that the two generals disagreed. De Gaulle ordered his representatives in NATO to warn the Supreme Commander that he had decided to remove his naval units in the Mediterranean from NATO control. They "would henceforth no longer be available in time of war." As political analyst David Schoenbrun pointed out, this meant either nothing at all or too much. If they were not available in time of war, what use could they be to NATO?

Eisenhower replied at the end of March, 1959, coming out for "the most complete and close co-operation within the NATO framework." During a press conference at the Élysée, De Gaulle made a public reply, drawing a distinction between the "unity" of the Western Alliance, which was desirable, and the "integration" of the various forces, which was not. As

Boileau wrote, "What is clearly conceived is clearly expressed." On that day, before the red-and-gold wainscoting of the Élysée, De Gaulle showed that he had a clear concept of what his future attitude would be.

Eisenhower was upset. He came to Paris in September and got a fantastically warm welcome from both the crowds and De Gaulle. De Gaulle was radiant. Ike was radiant. Since he might need the support of the United States, De Gaulle took advantage of the occasion to announce a change in his Algerian policy. Algeria would decide its future on its own; it would have self-determination. And, as he expected, the American Secretary of State, Christian Herter, asked the United Nations to do nothing to interfere with "such a courageous initiative."

But at the same time De Gaulle made it clear that no diplomatic support, no "veterans' reunion," would lead him to alter significantly his relations with America. In a speech at the École Militaire he stuck to his decision to have *his own* atomic bomb. He definitively put an end to the hope that France would integrate its forces automatically into those of NATO. "The system that has been known as integration . . . has outlived its use. . . . The nation's defense can only be a national defense." On the same occasion, De Gaulle announced that Khrushchev had accepted his invitation to come to France, and that he would arrive in Paris on March 15, 1960. In this way he showed the Anglo-Saxons that he would not leave them a monopoly on diplomatic action and dealings with the East any more than he would recognize their leadership in defensive strategy.

On De Gaulle's return visit to Eisenhower, on the banks of the Potomac and the Hudson, he made his everlasting claim that France was independent. He wanted France to be on an equal footing with Great Britain and the United States, since France was one of the three powers in the Free World with global responsibilities. Eisenhower, who was reaching the end of his term in office, refused to listen, and De Gaulle became more and more demanding. On September 5, he violently attacked NATO, declaring that henceforth France had to rely on itself, "for our only defense is our national defense."

He had finished with Eisenhower, who had anyway not long to go in office. When Kennedy took office in January of 1961, he received two particularly notable telegrams. One came from Khrushchev, who expressed the hope that American policy would return to what it had been under Roosevelt. The other came from General de Gaulle; it said that he was counting on the new generation "to take over the heavy responsibilities of leadership and to strengthen the ties of traditional friendship between the two countries." According to David Schoenbrun, Kennedy burst into laughter and exclaimed: "One thing is sure. I will not be able to satisfy both of them."

De Gaulle's telegram was at least a sign of France's increasing interest in the United States, and, indeed, in all foreign relations. When De Gaulle had to force other nations to recognize France's status in the world and to guarantee its possessions, he had shown concern mainly for France alone. His preoccupations were national, or, as some would say, nationalistic. Kennedy's election coincided with an improvement in France's position and with a new strength in its domestic affairs. This gave De Gaulle the opportunity to broaden his foreign policy. Not only would he be able to build up France in his own way; he would also be able to map a new course for the world with a stronger France at its head, a course that would attempt to solve its major problems and deadlocks. De Gaulle then began to ask openly the question that had worried him for twenty years, the question he had had ample time to think about during his retirement at Colombey-les-Deux-Églises: what would be the new course of the West now that France had recovered its sense of mission and its world initiative? Once again, De Gaulle revived the ancient political and religious notion *"Gesta Dei per Francos"* in his role as a monarch, or an imitation monarch. His ambitions grew; so did his difficulties in fulfilling, or even starting, his programs. It had been relatively easy to make world claims for France. It was far less easy to clarify and propose, if not impose, solutions to universal problems. Perhaps, in this area, the "doctrine" of Gaullism risks being most flawed and ambivalent.

IF I WERE PRESIDENT OF THE UNITED STATES . . .

For a time De Gaulle's tendency to apply his policies to the world took only the form of suggestions. But these suggestions became more frequent and more concrete, especially at each of De Gaulle's meetings with Kennedy in Paris in the early summer of 1961.

Colonel Passy (André Dewavrin), Director of the Free French Information Bureau in London for four years, has been close to De Gaulle for years. He described an incident which may shed light on De Gaulle's subsequent attitude toward Kennedy, an incident that took place in 1947.

De Gaulle had resigned from office the previous year and was about to found his party, the R.P.F. One of the reasons he wanted to return to public life as soon as possible was his belief that there would soon be a showdown between the U.S.S.R. and the United States. President Truman had taken a determined stand against the Soviets and had slammed his fist on the table over Russia's refusal to withdraw from Iran. He hinted that he would not back down even if the Russians threatened war. As he was then the sole possessor of the atomic bomb, he knew that he had the upper hand. At that time De Gaulle held several conversations with Colonel Passy, either in Colombey or in Paris. Though Passy does not tell in great detail in his *Memoirs* what went on during these meetings, he outlined the important factors for me.

In view of the dangerous international situation, De Gaulle

insisted that Passy join his *Rassemblement*. Passy refused for
two reasons. The first was that, because of France's domestic
politics, he thought the *Rassemblement* would be a mistake
which would unite the older political parties against De
Gaulle. The second and chief reason was that he did not believe there would be a war, for in spite of the firm stand Truman had taken, Truman could not, both for domestic and
international reasons, risk unleashing a major conflict. He
would not carry through with his threats.

When Passy had finished his argument, the General's face
hardened and the animation in his expression disappeared. He
was visibly impressed by Passy's reasoning. At the end of it,
his only answer was the exclamation "Oh, if only I were
President of the United States!"

He voiced this wish on the spur of the moment, when he
learned about certain restrictions on the President he had not
known previously. But at times he was probably tempted to
try to make this paradoxical and unrealistic wish come true.
De Gaulle has never pretended to run the White House; but
from the room in Blair House where he has often stayed, and
from the Élysée, where he speaks on equal terms with American presidents, he might have felt he could influence them,
especially Kennedy.

This may be the reason for his exceptional interest in
Eisenhower's successor and the particular attention he paid to
the new President. It also explains, probably, why he felt so
deeply the tragedy of Kennedy's death.

He was grateful to Kennedy for his youth, his open-
mindedness and, phrasing it negatively, for the absence of any
stiffness in his personality. When Kennedy was a Senator, he
energetically denounced France's Algerian policy at a time
when France wished to maintain the *status quo*. Although
this tempestuous outburst on the Senator's part had provoked
hostile reactions in France, De Gaulle could not help but

note that Kennedy had merely anticipated the evolution of his own future policies.

And so, when Kennedy became President of the United States, De Gaulle began to play the role of mentor for the first time. He approved of the young man who had reached power so young, and he was ready to aid the "New World" with his advice and experience and to give the novice statesman the benefit of his deep thought on the future politics of the world. It was wonderful to see how patient and persistent he was in his talks with Kennedy from May 30 to June 2, 1961, in which he brought up the crucial points of world politics that concerned both France and the United States. He announced that he was satisfied with the American policy over Berlin. He lavished advice on Laos, where he counseled nonintervention. Making use of the dearly-acquired military experience of the French generals, he advised Kennedy not to begin the same hideous cycle in Vietnam. The two vital points of difference in the relationship between the two republics were NATO and the French atomic bomb, and there the two men disagreed. De Gaulle allowed Kennedy to give a detailed analysis of the reasons why France should give up its nuclear striking force; he then forced Kennedy to sit through a précis of contemporary history, through much of which he had lived himself. The conclusion of this lecture was that NATO would have to be reorganized so that France could play a leading part in it.

In their two-day discussions, De Gaulle never abandoned his magisterial tone, which he felt was justified by his age and by his past. His manner was grandfatherly. On the occasions when Mrs. Kennedy acted as interpreter at these sessions, her youth and charm obviously worked their spell on the General and lent an atmosphere of intimacy to the meetings. Nonetheless, De Gaulle was not inclined to reveal his secrets to Kennedy. When the two men parted, the American President asked the question that all their previous conversations had hinted at: "For fifty years now, you have been dedicating yourself to becoming what a head of state ought to be. Is there anything you have found out that I ought to know?" De Gaulle promised that he would tell him the answer another time, when he was in less of a hurry. But perhaps he could have been heard muttering, as he left, the words he had said to Passy, "Oh, if only I were President of the United States!" Kennedy was probably a bit disappointed. He is said to have made the airy remark, "If I have to wait too long for his answer, I'll probably know as much as he does."

Kennedy's assassination put an end to all that. Without wasting any time, De Gaulle got in touch with President Johnson after Kennedy's funeral. De Gaulle had met Johnson once, in December, 1960. Apparently, Johnson reminds him of Truman in some ways, and not only because both men were Vice-Presidents called on to become President. He appreciates the practical mind and the grip on reality of both men.

"Johnson," De Gaulle was to say, "is not a politician; he is a political man." Coming from him, no praise can be higher. Johnson has also sized up the General in a humorous way: "De Gaulle isn't at all like the descriptions of him. I was told that he was cold and starchy. I found him extremely warm, a bit of a *grand seigneur*, in the elegant way of the Old South. And I discovered that we actually did have something in common, our height. We are both about six feet four inches tall. We can see things eye to eye."*

The conclusion to all this is that De Gaulle's dealings with the Americans pose a problem different from his dealings with the English. He admires the nobility of the English tradition and national courage and pride, even when it is used against him. Men, after all, matter little, except as momentary cata-

* From "De Gaulle and the Anglo-Saxons," by David Schoenbrun, *Le Figaro,* July 9, 1964.

lysts on a field of unchanging forces. Some are more receptive than others. Some loom larger than others. But from Churchill to Wilson, the firm is the same and so is the product, tested over the centuries.

On the other hand, De Gaulle has no a priori attitude toward the United States. He knows that each American president—within limits, of course—can put a different stamp on his country's policies. Kennedy was not like Eisenhower, any more than Johnson is like Roosevelt. At the beginning of every presidential term, De Gaulle, that obstinate and patient fighter, has another chance to get a part of what he wants.

Apparently, then, it is through the United States rather than through Great Britain that De Gaulle will be able to rejoin and stay within the Western Alliance. Among his first-class allies, America, with each new president, seems the most likely to rejuvenate and relaunch the alliance.

DE GAULLE AND THE RUSSIANS

De Gaulle is often brutal and unbearable to his super-allies and his first-class allies, but he does not leave their camp. With his "enemy-allies" and his second-class allies, on the contrary, he is often amiable; but he is also deceitful and wily. The Kremlin knows this well, and its branch in Paris, the French Communist party, knows it too.

De Gaulle has often been reproached for being the man who, in 1944 and 1945, put Communists in his Cabinet. He is also blamed for making an alliance with Stalin and for allowing Maurice Thorez to return to France to become a minister and a member of the government. According to this interpretation, De Gaulle has played the Russian game inside and outside France—at least in appearance. Since he is also beginning to negotiate with the Kremlin now in the same way he did twenty years ago with Stalin, he runs the risk of arousing the same suspicions and the same misunderstanding.

The belief that De Gaulle was or is pro-Russian, either in 1944 or today, is totally false. If he embraces the Communists or their masters, it is in order to wind them. If he appears to make concessions to them, it is all the better to neutralize them. He does not give way on essentials and he never will.

After France was liberated, between June, 1944, and May, 1945, the Communists posed a great threat to De Gaulle's government. Ever since July, 1941, they had played an important part in the struggle against Vichy and in the Resistance against the Germans. They threatened certain regions and some large cities, such as Limoges, Toulouse, Montpellier, and Bordeaux, where their military or paramilitary organizations, called the Milices Patriotiques, were well armed, well trained, and ready to take action as soon as ordered to begin subversion.

In fact, De Gaulle's government in Algiers had set up an administrative machine to control any revolution after the Liberation of France. As soon as the Germans left, this machine, the *Commissaires de la République et Préfets*, was to take up its posts in France to keep order in the ensuing chaos. De Gaulle also had his own representatives in France, distinct from those of the Resistance, who were to neutralize the Communist elements in its ranks. Among these, Alexander Parodi was to play an important part during the liberation of Paris. And the two Communist ministers in De Gaulle's Cabinet did not, in spite of the pressure of their party, get the key posts which would have given them undue influence in the government. They did not control the Ministry of the Interior, Foreign Affairs, or the War Ministry. The most they obtained, in April, 1944, after months of negotiations, was an honorific position in ministries that had no power. François Billoux was made Under Secretary of State, and F. J. Grenier was made Under Secretary of Aviation, which meant practically nothing at all, since at that time, all French airplanes were under Allied command. In September

DE GAULLE AND HIS ALLIES /167

of 1944, Grenier was replaced by Charles Tillon; Billoux took over the innocuous Ministry of Public Health.

DE GAULLE PAYS STALIN A VISIT

In order to neutralize the Stalinists for good, De Gaulle had to get the Milices Patriotiques dissolved. The French Communists would never agree to such a step, so De Gaulle turned to Moscow. He met with Stalin in December, 1944. Thorez returned to France almost immediately afterward.

Step by step, De Gaulle, supported by the French Communists, maneuvered at the expense of his second-class ally. On November 27, 1944, Thorez was allowed to return to Paris. Three days later, he spoke in public for the first time at the Vélodrome d'Hiver, where he delivered such vague and moderate instructions that the militant Communists were astounded. This was a turning point in the party's policy.

A month earlier, on October 27, 1944, Jacques Duclos had launched an appeal for an increased recruiting program for the Milices Patriotiques. Thorez simply came out with a few generalized and mild slogans, such as, "Declare war," "Create a powerful French army," "Rapidly reconstruct industry," "Unite." Many wondered what had happened to Thorez in Moscow, or what was going to happen, since he no longer spoke as a militant on his return to France.

On January 21, 1945, people began to understand. After De Gaulle's lengthy stay in Moscow, the Central Committee of the French Communist party had met at Ivry, where Thorez delivered his report. To everyone's surprise, he declared himself against the continued existence of the Milices or of the Gardes Patriotiques. "Those armed groups had reason to exist before and during the Occupation, against the Hitlerian invaders and their Vichyite accomplices. But the situation is different now. Public security must be enforced by the regular police forces specifically appointed for that task. Civil guards, and *all* irregular armed groups, should not be kept any longer."

And so the Communist shock troops were disbanded by the Secretary General of the party himself. Everything occurred as though Thorez, by pronouncing these words, were repaying De Gaulle for his return to France and for the Franco-Soviet pact.

There was little in the pact that justified such a sacrifice. It contained a few general clauses which are always found in documents of this sort, and which, experience shows, are not always observed. It provided for the continuation of the common struggle against Germany, and for various agreements. France and Russia were not to conclude any separate peace treaty or armistice. They were to adopt common measures for the prevention of any future German aggression. Neither was to join any coalition or alliance directed against the other. They were to grant each other reciprocal economic assistance. And all treaties with a third party concluded by either nation were to be compatible with the said treaty. This treaty was to last for twenty years.

There was nothing in it which bothered De Gaulle. On only one point had Stalin tried to draw him into an engagement that would commit the General to Stalin's side. The issue in question was Poland. That country was still largely occupied by the Germans and was represented by two governments in exile. The first was in London and on the side of the West; the second, the so-called Lublin Committee, had pledged allegiance to the Russians. Both had armies fighting against the Germans on the Eastern and the Western fronts.

Stalin wanted De Gaulle to recognize the Lublin Committee, even arranged for the General to meet its leaders. De Gaulle received them at the French Embassy and got "a poor impression" of them. They were partisans "evidently under the orders of the Communists, merely mouthing couplets that had been prepared for them."

De Gaulle persisted in his refusal, Stalin continued to insist. One final sumptuous dinner brought the negotiators together. Stalin used every means of seduction and pressure to obtain recognition for his men, but seeing that they had reached a deadlock, De Gaulle suddenly took his leave at midnight. He spoke a few courteous diplomatic phrases and left, saying, "Goodbye, Marshal," to Stalin. Molotov, who had arranged the meeting, was flabbergasted, pale and stuttering. Those present could find nothing to say. Stalin immediately held a meeting with his staff to "reconsider the situation." At 2:00 A.M., he yielded. After last-minute talks, the treaty was signed at four o'clock that morning. De Gaulle had not given in, and after this interlude, the dinner began again.

There was only one threat uttered that night. Stalin said to his unfortunate interpreter, who had had good reason to be present all the time: "As for you, you know too much. I'm tempted to send you to Siberia."

When De Gaulle returned to France, he did not have to worry about the false and misleading interpretations of his reasons for signing the pact. By utter stubbornness and subtle diplomacy, he had achieved his goal, which was to eliminate the Communist menace in France. He had given away nothing of any value to the Soviet camp. He had also succeeded in worrying his Anglo-Saxon allies.

This model of great diplomacy was the work of one man's genius. Its disadvantage was that its success could not be declared or explained. It aroused the anger and the defiance of the very people who were defended by its terms and who should have been prejudiced in its favor. Every element in France that opposed the Russians should have acclaimed him. Yet most of them still believe that De Gaulle played into Stalin's hands. The truth should be remembered, now that the General is starting on another diplomatic game with Khrushchev's successors and with his new "enemy-allies" in Peking.

KHRUSHCHEV'S VISIT TO DE GAULLE

The good use which De Gaulle made of his trip to the U.S.S.R. and of the pact of 1944 is now clear. Sixteen years later it was Stalin's successor who took the trouble to visit the General in Paris, much to the surprise of De Gaulle's first-class allies. This sensational initiative put the General's future policy and new maneuvers in question.

He had certainly not become more sympathetic toward the Russians or the French Stalinists since 1945. On the contrary, his attitude toward them had hardened on many occasions. At Rennes, on July 27, 1947, he pronounced French Communists beyond the pale, branding them as "separatists." "At a time when the future of our nation is in danger," the General had declared, "when a huge Eastern bloc is being created in Europe by force, the sole reaction of these people is to support in our midst, exclusively and loudly, only the positions, only the intentions, and only the interests of Soviet Russia."*

At Bourges, on February 25, 1951, he expounded the same theme. The United States had disappointed De Gaulle again: it had dropped the idea of spreading the Korean conflict to China. "It is now eight months," De Gaulle announced, "since war began. Doubtless, it is limited for the moment to distant parts of Asia. Doubtless, men of good will have not lost the hope of mastering the scourge. The prospect of extending the war gives rise to anxiety everywhere and influences every action. . . . Within our frontiers, Communist organizations flourish. . . . Beyond our frontiers, the Soviet menace grows. . . . Our Atlantic allies are not making plans for an effective defense of this old continent, should there be an invasion."†

After his return to power, De Gaulle's attitude altered. It

---

* Joseph Barsalon, *La Mal Aimée* (Paris: Plon, 1964).
† Paul-Marie de la Gorce, *De Gaulle entre Deux Mondes* (Paris: Librairie Arthème Fayard, 1964), p. 498.

was not that his feelings had changed toward Marxism or toward those who, in France or elsewhere, defended its internationalist, materialistic, and atheistic creed. But political necessity led him to suspend his hostility and to transform his former enemies into second-class allies. During a press conference on March 25, 1959, he declared that he considered the German-Polish frontier fixed forever on the Oder and the Neisse. This decision was not likely to please his German ally or the West. During the same year he struck another note of discord. He stated that Red China had to be recognized as a powerful and independent nation.

What were the reasons for these actions—which hardly seem gratuitous?

First of all, De Gaulle appeared to be playing domestic politics. Since 1958 he had no longer been a leader of the Opposition. He had returned to power. Perhaps, in these very different circumstances, he might need to put pressure on the French Communists, who would follow the orders of Moscow as in 1944. Who knows if the General, who looks far ahead, may have reckoned even then that, in the case of a referendum or the renewal of his seven-year term as President, he would need the votes of the Communists? At that time, his having been all smiles with Moscow and on nodding terms with Peking would look very good on election day. But foreign policy considerations must also have played their part, different as they are when dealing with Moscow or with Peking. By starting negotiations with Russia again, De Gaulle hoped to win increased recognition of France's importance in world affairs. Already, on November 10, 1959, at a press conference he predicted the way in which the Communist nations would develop and the certainty of a break between China and the U.S.S.R. He also predicted that, because Russia had reached a nuclear stalemate with the United States, France might play a special part as a mediator between the two countries and thus relieve world tension.

On May 14 and 15, 1960, during a summit conference in

Paris bringing together Macmillan, De Gaulle, Khrushchev, and Eisenhower, he was able to translate these words into acts. The horizon, or at least the Russian horizon, did not look bright before the meeting opened. It was no coincidence that on the previous day Sputnik IV, weighing four and a half tons, had flashed across the sky. It was launched to impress the other members of the conference and to display Russia's progress in the field of outer space. There was also, perhaps, no coincidence in the fact that one of the American reconnaissance planes had been shot down by the Russians while flying indiscreetly but peacefully over Communist territory. The incident was very convenient for Khrushchev. American Intelligence did not know that the pilot was alive and that he had confessed to everything, and they began, therefore, by denying the facts that they would later have to admit. Khrushchev exploited the incident to present Eisenhower with a form of ultimatum: he demanded that the United States declare in public that it had stopped its flights over Russia. Eisenhower answered that "the flights have been suspended and shall not be undertaken again." Khrushchev then asked how long this promise would hold, and Eisenhower answered: "During the time that I am President of the United States," which only meant, "Until the end of the year." The Soviet Premier did not consider this reply satisfactory, and after a session lasting forty-eight hours the conference broke up.

The failure of this meeting defeated De Gaulle's own policy. It prevented France from playing the world role he had chosen for it.

DE GAULLE AND COMMUNIST CHINA

With Communist China, De Gaulle pursues the same policy he does with Russia, although of course the political context is quite different.

Doubtless one of his motives for recognizing Mao Tse-tung

was economic, for like England, Denmark, and Norway, France was restoring normal diplomatic relations with a country that contained an immense reservoir of men and of wealth. But for De Gaulle, who is constantly preoccupied with world politics, it meant much more than that.

When he announced his intention of recognizing Mao Tse-tung's regime, on January 27, 1964, during another press conference, it was because he was once again hoping to play a role worthy of himself and of his country.

He was reviving the ambitions of every statesman in France since 1940, of whatever political origin. It had even been the ambition of Pierre Laval, who hoped to act as intermediary between Germany and the Allies, and who wanted to remedy the real weakness of France's position by the subtlety of his diplomatic negotiations. De Gaulle also wants to play the part of mediator, of intercessor or interpreter between the two blocs, superior to France in actual power, but inferior, according to him, in historical experience. He wants to serve as the go-between of the West, under American leadership, and the Far Eastern countries, where France has gained its costly but precious experience over seventy-five years.

Only the future can decide whether the General's dream is more realistic than Pierre Laval's. For the moment, the one thing which can be known for certain is that De Gaulle's recognition of Red China was not only to kowtow to the mandarins.

CHAPTER IV

Gaullism as a Doctrine

It is evident from De Gaulle's dealings with his allies that as a statesman he operates on two different levels.

In the short term, he constantly stresses a rather short-sighted nationalism of the Maurras type, probably because of his origins and upbringing. His behavior is sometimes anachronistic.

But in the long term, he shows concern for the future of Western civilization and for the cultural entity that Europe represents *in saecula saeculorum*. He deals with the daily incidents of history as they crop up. But he is more preoccupied with the long-range problems raised by the civilization of today, in which two apparently incompatible concepts of life confront one another.

It is as though he looks at politics and history through bifocal lenses. Or rather, he is like the driver of a car who, in order to avoid an accident, has to look out for bumps and ruts in the road and objects that might get under his wheels at the same time that he has to look before him as far as he can down the road, all the way to the horizon.

The question is whether De Gaulle, with the double vision of a statesman, is able to calculate both distances correctly. Is he able to avoid nearby obstacles and at the same time reach his distant goal? Since the nearby goal is nationalism, perhaps he misses or forgets the distant one, his dream of internationalism.

That is De Gaulle's major risk. If he were to fall into that trap, it would be the great mistake of his life.

Is Gaullism a passing phenomenon?

The General's secrets and mysteries have been examined. His attitude toward power, his personal behavior, and his particular method of dealing with life and people have all been explored as objectively as possible. It is time for an analysis of the General's place in history, the impact of his political actions, and their chances of survival. Twenty years ago in Algiers, "President" Edgar Faure claimed that Gaullism was only a passing phenomenon. No one knows whether he was right or wrong.

At any rate, it is still not clear if the regime founded by the General is a Gaullist one or merely De Gaulle's. Is Gaullism the work of one man, who, however hard he tries to make a legacy of his policies, will not succeed in perpetuating them beyond his own lifetime? Or does De Gaulle express a coherent doctrine, adapted to the needs of our time? If the latter is true, Gaullism has every chance of surviving to influence the future, even after De Gaulle's death.

The problems of liberty

The problem confronting the Free European countries, and specifically confronting De Gaulle if he wishes to consolidate his glory, is to restore prestige to governments committed to freedom. The American system is a century and a half old and is now growing out of date. The doctrine of the Soviet system is one century old and has been in operation for half that time. It, too, is beginning to break down. De Gaulle's task is to find institutions for the Free World that are adapted to our age. The Free World must again take the initiative and resolve the difficulties that for thirty years have eclipsed the democracies in the face of totalitarianism.

The problem is to know what these difficulties are and where they originate.

One of the difficulties is a parliamentary system that has become synonymous with inefficiency and instability in all the free countries, with the possible exception of Great Britain, Belgium, and Holland—which, paradoxically, have kept a monarchy. By functioning normally, the parliamentary system has paved the way for dictatorships during the past fifty years. The Italian Parliament gave birth to Mussolini's regime; the German one aided Hitler. This must mean that there is something wrong with the system in the first place. The actual concept of a parliament and of a deputy's role as the representative of the people, in France and in the other Free European countries, is an anomalous, incoherent, and even absurd doctrine.

After all, what *is* a deputy in the parliamentary regimes which still exist in Europe?

Practically speaking, there are three possible interpretations of a deputy's role. Each assigns the deputy different rights. They are also different because, historically, each took over where the previous one left off.

It is said that the deputy is the people's representative. More precisely, this means that he is, first of all, the authorized agent of those who have elected him. Secondly, he is the authorized agent of the whole nation. Thirdly, he is a temporary civil servant, bound by contract to the state.

In the first case, he represents his constituency. He is responsible to it for his activity in parliament and for the way he defends the interests of those who have sent him there.

In the second case, although elected by his constituency, he is also the tribune of the entire nation. He must try to make laws which are good for all, even if this means sacrificing those who elected him.

In the third case, although elected by a constituency, he becomes a servant of the state by virtue of the people's vote. In this role he must carry out public and legislative duties in the name of the state until his term expires.

If the deputy were able to choose one of these three attitudes, the nature of his functions would in no way be equivocal. But in fact his activity is determined by all three concepts. He is a hybrid. He belongs to his electors, to his country, and to his state. And it does not help matters that he also belongs to his party. It is an impossible position, made evident by the confusion and impotence of the parliamentary systems of Europe.

Historically, these three ideas of the deputy's role grew up successively in France and in the other nations of the West. The fact that they did succeed one another proves that they were not then confused.

In the States-General of the French monarchies, the deputy was considered only the representative of his electorate. He was wholly bound to do what his constituency wished. Beyond the mandate approved by his electors, he had no right to act on his own initiative.

This was clear in 1319, at Poitiers, when Philip V asked the States-General for subsidies after consulting them on the matters for which they had been summoned. The deputies had been given no mandate to grant new taxes. They asked to consult their electors first, and after doing so, returned a few months later to give their refusal. It is inconceivable that a deputy today would ask to consult his constituents before voting in Parliament on some question not included in his election platform. Such an action would seem anachronistic, for the representative mandate has replaced the binding one. The decisive moment for this take-over was at the beginning of the convocation of the States-General under Louis XVI. The King called the binding mandate "unconstitutional" and against the interests of the state. This severed the ties linking the deputies to their electors. Above all it ushered in the revolutionary constitutions. All of them, including the Constitution of 1791 and the Jacobin Constitution of 1793, declared that "each deputy belongs to the entire nation." Under them the deputies were to prepare referendums which would ratify the proposals they had passed in Parliament.

The third concept of a deputy's role, as an offshoot of the state, was the result of the Constitution of the Year VIII, for which the Abbé Sieyés was responsible. The Constitution declared that those who were to represent the people should be selected by the state or the government. The voters would cast ballots for a list of notable men, and the Senate would choose its members from these lists. It would also choose the members of the legislative body and the Tribunal, while the government chose the State Councilors. During this period a phrase was coined that could be adopted by all authoritarian regimes: "Trust must come from below, and power must come from above."

Today the confusion over the deputy's role is total. His function is an inextricable mixture of all the theories that have successively flowered in France.

He belongs to his electors, and the way most deputies stick to their mandate shows them to be timid imitators of the old-style French deputies. They kowtow to those constituents who want some decoration or unjustified promotion, yet they often put the interests of their constituency second when they vote on matters of national importance. For the deputy also belongs to his country, since his election enables him, by the use of his vote, to make and change laws for the nation as a whole. And, more ambiguously still, each deputy also belongs to a "national," therefore centralized, party. The deputy is also a civil servant, at least by contract, for the elected deputy owns his seat for four years, whether his constituents still want him or not.

What, then, is a deputy in Europe today? He is everything and at the same time nothing. He is everything because he looks after the welfare and the rights of his local constituency, his country, and his state, as well as his party. He is nothing because he is unable to choose between his various functions.

He is the geometrical center of all the conflicts and contradictions which a country must inevitably bear when it is over-centralized and when all power is held by a central government. In most European countries there are no states like those of the United States or like the *Länder* in Germany, which keep some authority from the nation's capital. To believe in the independence and the moral virtues of a deputy one would have to take for granted that local, state, and national interest never need be in conflict. But this would be rank optimism.

Conflicts of interest can be fruitful—but only when different interests are represented by different organisms and different people. When the same person has to look out for all interests, he naturally becomes confused, ineffectual, and compromising, whatever his good qualities. If the deputies have become unpopular, it is not because they lack personal qualities or because they are dishonest: it is because the system puts them in an impossible situation. There is a congestion of all the real powers which properly belong all over the nation; they accumulate in the center and devolve on the same men and the same organisms.

In his time, Montesquieu based democracy on the separation of powers. Perhaps De Gaulle, in our time, will be able to save democracy by insuring the separation of its functions. He has sensed the nature of the problem; but will he be able to, will he want to, and will he know how to solve it?

De Gaulle has also sensed, at least partially, a second problem. In the field of international relations there is such total confusion concealed under a veneer of meaning that no one knows what the issues really are. This confusion has lasted for over a century. Its pattern of development, at least, is easy to trace. The "fatherland" and the "nation" are two distinct notions; but they have been confused, often by De Gaulle himself.

The historical reasons for such an error throw some light on the confusion. The fate of Europe was determined a century ago. It was then that countries such as Italy and Germany were deciding how to form themselves into a single unit. They hesitated between the strategy of war and the strategy of negotiation and peace. They did not know whether they would need a centralized state—a Jacobin and indivisible "nation"—or a loose federation of all the various local "fatherlands"—the free cities, the regions, the little kingdoms and the duchies which had made up the country until that time. Under the latter system, each little fatherland would keep its prerogatives, its institutions, and its independent existence. The planners did not know whether to set up a Europe of nations—in other words, a Europe of great imperialisms—or a Europe of fatherlands, of independent countries who associated to guarantee each other's freedoms, respect each other's customs, consent to an equal partnership that would triumph over temporary difficulties. The choice these new nations then made would be decisive for the future of Europe. The novelty and urgency of that choice was fully obvious to the men of the time and made them anxious. Unfortunately, their anxiety was fully justified.

A Belgian economist, Émile de Laveleye, wrote the following in 1868: "I confess that it is not without deep emotion that I bring up the question of nationalities. I am convinced that, ultimately, nationalism will further the progress of civilization; yet, nonetheless, it worries me and sometimes fills me with anxiety. . . . It turns treaties into a mockery and puts an end to historic rights. It throws diplomacy into a turmoil, shakes every foundation, alarms all interests, and it may, in the future, bring about world war."*

Two years later, on September 15, 1870, Joseph Renan would echo his anguish. At the beginning of the conflict between France and Germany, when the threat of Prussian nationalism was being felt for the first time by France, Renan

* *Revue des Deux Mondes,* August 1, 1868.

wrote: "The principle of independent nationalities is not likely, as many think, to deliver the human species from the scourge of war. On the contrary, I have always been afraid that the principle of nationalism, as a substitute for the mild and paternalistic symbol of legitimacy, may cause the wars between peoples to degenerate into the extermination of races. It will strike from the code of human rights the moderation and courtesy possible in the small political and dynastic wars of the past."*

Unfortunately, except for a few words, these lines could have been written today. But the words that Proudhon wrote, ten years before that, are even more timely. The great French Socialist who opposed Karl Marx and fathered the doctrine of Federal Socialism, foresaw the risks of dictatorship that threatened the European countries under the cloak of nationalism. He predicted that dictatorship would rule in Germany and Italy should those countries become nations rather than federated fatherlands.

Sixty years before the event he anticipated Fascism in Italy. "The system of nationalism," he wrote, "can lead to nothing but a new despotism, a despotism such as Italy has not known since the time of Caesar." "Germany," he wrote, "is looking for a federation. Woe to the world if it should fall into the rut of centralism."†

In a more generalized fashion he predicted that, in this century, the world would risk terrible catastrophes if it blindly set out to endorse the principle of nationality. "The twentieth century will begin an age of federation or plunge humanity into another purgatory lasting a thousand years."

And so, Europe in the middle of the nineteenth century was aware of its choice. Italy and Germany would have to choose either an association of provinces, counties, regions,

* Joseph Renan, *La Reforme Intellectuelle et Morale* (London: Cambridge, 1950).
† Pierre Proudhon, *Correspondence*, Vol. XI, letter of April 21, 1861, to Aleksandr Herzen.

and fatherlands, each preserving its independence within a freely constituted association, or the centralization of the unified state, a path that would lead to the totalitarianism of Bismarck and Cavour.

The same problem exists today, if not on a world scale, at least on a European scale. Again, a choice must be made, either between a federation of free countries, a federation of fatherlands each keeping its independence, or under the brutal hegemony of a monolithic and imperialist state, such as China or the U.S.S.R.; or the hegemony of a more humane and liberal nation like the United States.

Basically, De Gaulle must decide among these choices, but he has not yet chosen, or rather, his choices have been contradictory.

The General knows very well that two problems confront the Western democracies: domestic problems, which demand a new distribution of functions within the framework of the free countries; and diplomatic problems, which demand new relationships between associated countries.

He is known to have read Laveleye, Renan, and Proudhon. He is sure to have read a more recent, and vitally important, text, the papal encyclical *Pacem in Terris*.

He has been warned. He knows that the salvation of the Western democracies does not rest solely on their subtle diplomatic maneuvers or on the strength of their nuclear weapons. What is needed first and foremost is a lucidity and firmness in their ideas on politics and a readiness to invent new forms of government. Europe, the Europe of fatherlands, and specifically France, must try to work out a new system of government—and substitute it for the obsolete ideologies of Russia and the United States.

TWO ESSENTIAL TEXTS OF GAULLISM

We turn to two essential texts for a definition of the General's political doctrine. The first is a speech delivered in

Brazzaville on January 30, 1944, at the opening of a conference to define the new direction of French policy toward its
African territories. The second is the speech made at Bayeux
on June 16, 1947, to prepare for the Constitution of the Gaullist *Rassemblement.*

Both these texts are actually manifestoes. At many other
times and in many other speeches De Gaulle has hidden, or at
least partially concealed, his ideas. But at Brazzaville and at
Bayeux he said what he thought. Before taking two decisive
steps he committed himself, not only before his listeners, but
also before history.

Both these texts attempt to give a partial reply to the two
fundamental questions that face Western democracy.

The vital parts of the Bayeux speech, concerning the internal structure of democracy, are these:

It is clear and it goes without saying that the final vote on laws
and budgets is the task of an Assembly that has been elected by
universal and direct suffrage. But the initiatives of such an Assembly may not necessarily be farsighted or wholly certain. Therefore a second Assembly, elected and set up in a different manner,
should be given the task of reconsidering in public what the first
one has passed. This second Assembly would also decide on appointments, and propose other laws. Although the great currents
of national politics are naturally reflected within the Chamber of
Deputies, local life also has its trends and its rights. It has rights
in the Saar, which, by the nature of our victory, once more takes
its place beside us, the sons of France. The future of 110 million
men and women, living under our flag, lies in the organization of
a form of federalism, which in time will emerge more clearly. But
our new Constitution must mark its beginnings and further its
development.

Everything, then, points to the formation of a second chamber;
its members will, on the whole, be elected by our general and
municipal councilors. This chamber will complement the main
one by making it revise its projects if necessary, and by considering
other ones. It would bring about an element of administrative
order in the making of laws, which an assembly—elected for

purely political reasons—necessarily tends to neglect. One of its normal features will be the inclusion of representatives of economic, domestic, and intellectual organizations, so that the voice of the nation's great activities will be heard within the state itself. With the members of the local assemblies and of the overseas territories, the members of this assembly will make up a great Council of the French Union, qualified to examine the laws and the problems that concern the Union: its budgets, its foreign relations, its internal issues, its national defense, its economy, and its communications.

It goes without saying that the Parliament, made up of two chambers and wielding legislative power, cannot wield executive power as well. This would lead to a confusion in powers that would soon change the government into nothing more than a gathering of delegations. . . . Therefore, it must be the head of state who will wield executive power. The head of state will be above parties, chosen by an electoral college which includes the Parliament, but which is much larger and composed in such a way as to make him the president of the French Union as well as the president of the Republic.

It will be the head of state's task to decide what is the national interest when it comes to choosing his men, taking into consideration the general trend in Parliament. It will be his function to name ministers and, first of all, of course, to choose the premier who will direct policy and the work of the government. It will be the head of state's function to promulgate laws and to make decrees. . . .

What distinguishes this vital speech is De Gaulle's desire to eliminate the confusion which had previously ruled the parliamentary system. By his scheme, executive power was taken away from the deputies or from the ministries they controlled. It was to be exercised by the head of state. Also, the elected deputies would represent only the political opinions of their electors; the professional, economic, intellectual, and domestic interests were to have other representatives in a distinct Assembly. The second Assembly would be appointed by other means than the popular ballot. Finally, the French Union would also have its own special representatives.

This was the beginning of a true Restoration, although the word was perhaps not used. For a hundred years, democracy had been synonymous with centralization, unification, and sometimes confusion. De Gaulle wanted to give free play to the forces that made up democracy and to restore their equilibrium. He abandoned the Jacobin concept of a unitarian state and proposed a new concept, that of federalism. He proposed the association and the organization of different powers and freedoms.

The Brazzaville speech had already shown clearly enough that this decentralization of powers would be extended to the countries of the French Union. Until then they had been governed by metropolitan France, and decisions were made in Paris. But now they too would enjoy the benefits of autonomy, while awaiting independence.

De Gaulle had been categorical on this point. He had said:

We believe that, as far as the world of tomorrow is concerned, autarchy will be neither desirable nor possible for anyone.

In French Africa, as in all the other territories where men live under our flag, there would be no progress if men, on their native soil . . . could not raise themselves, little by little, to the level where they were able to participate in the management of their countries and their own affairs.

If the two speeches are juxtaposed, the result is curious.

On the one hand, De Gaulle seemed determined to give special representation, free play, and autonomy back to all the various groups in France and the French Union. He went very far in this direction, since he took a general principle from his analysis of French politics and the politics of its territories. That principle was that self-sufficiency in the world of tomorrow would be impossible.

But at the same time, he thought that emancipation had to

be granted within the framework of the existing government, although that same framework had prevented emancipation until then. He wanted to keep Parliament, its structure, and its customs; all he wanted to change was the way its members would be chosen. He did not assume that the emancipation of the overseas territories might one day lead to their refusal to live under the French flag.

In this speech De Gaulle already revealed a hesitation in his arguments and a schism in his ideas.

THE HESITATIONS OF GAULLISM

In the constitution De Gaulle submitted to the vote on his return to power in 1958, little that was essential remained of the doctrine expressed at Bayeux. The division of functions and powers among specialized assemblies, each representing the live forces of the country and each expressing itself independently, was entirely forgotten. De Gaulle's constitution did not go to the heart of the parliamentary problem; it only dealt with Parliament's superficial weaknesses. It guaranteed governmental stability; or rather, it reduced the government's instability by initiating new electoral methods. It did not transform the structure of politics. It did nothing to end the basic confusion in the system of representation and in the functions of the deputy. When De Gaulle had consolidated the power of the executive and acquired it for himself as head of the state under a system of election different from that of the deputies, he thought that he had done enough to ensure the stability of his regime.

In the short term he was right. But he was wrong in view of the future. In the short term a very unusual thing happened, which had nothing to do with any constitution. For the first time France sent to Parliament an unconditional majority in favor of the government. This abnormal event was due solely to De Gaulle's personal prestige and made any constitution almost unnecessary. If the same thing had happened during the Third and the Fourth Republics, those regimes would have become models of stability, and Joseph Laniel might be in power to this day.

The fact that there is a stable government today has almost nothing to do with the clauses in the Constitution of the Fifth Republic. There is stability only because the voters have sent a Gaullist majority to Parliament; the electorate wanted the opposition in the minority, unable to overthrow the government.

But suppose that, before or after De Gaulle's death, this exceptional situation comes to an end. Suppose that, at the next election, the opposition parties return to Parliament with a majority, or at least numerous enough to prevent a majority from forming without them. In that case, all the old games will start again, with different rules. There will be instability in spite of all the clauses designed to prevent it. There will always be men in France clever enough to evade constitutional clauses which interfere with their intrigues or hamper their interests.

De Gaulle has done nothing except pull out temporary palliatives to counter the internal crises of the parliamentary system. These palliatives are linked to his prestige and his personal authority. They resolve nothing permanently. Any day the future can become threatening again, because of the uncertainty in his ideas which prevents him from doing those things which he desires most.

The same holds true of his foreign policy.

De Gaulle is one of the only statesmen today to analyze the problems of our age clearly. He was one of the first, if not the first, to point out the role that a united Europe could play between the two great rival nations of the U.S.S.R. and the U.S.A. As early as July 28, 1946, in a speech delivered at Bar-le-Duc, he declared:

Henceforth, no one can be exempt from the deep anxiety that weighs on every country and every individual because of the future relations between America and Russia.

Who can restore the balance between the two New Worlds, if not the Old World? Ancient Europe, which for so many centuries has guided the universe, is in a position to provide the necessary element of moderation and understanding in the heart of a world that is tending to split in half. . . . Before a harmony of this sort can be achieved, there will first have to be an understanding between London and Paris.

The last sentence of this speech may provoke a rather melancholy smile, but the rest of it holds true today.

It was necessary then, and it is still necessary, for Europeans to unite so that the world can regain its equilibrium. Yet there is one fact to bear in mind: the General has opposed, and, when he could, has destroyed every major effort made for nearly twenty years to establish European co-operation.

There are two reasons for this. One is a question of doctrine, the other of prestige and interest.

As far as doctrine is concerned, De Gaulle is evidently committed to the principle of nationality: he is a nationalist. For him, the nation represents the ultimate essential virtue of political life. He therefore accepts nothing that could curb the prerogatives and rights of the nation.

With the impetus of Robert Schuman, a treaty setting up the European Coal and Steel Community (C.E.C.A.) was signed in 1951. In 1957, the constitutions of the Common Market and of Euratom were drawn up. In opposition to De Gaulle's nationalism, the whole European structure presupposes that the six member nations of the Common Market will yield some of their sovereignty to a supranational organization. Therefore De Gaulle is hostile to it, for exactly the same reasons that he opposed the European Defense Community: it grouped nearly all the national armies into one European army. As we know, it failed.

And so the nation, which is the only reality, refuses to abdicate any of its rights. At most, a nation can join a confederation of other nations, instead of joining a federal system and yielding some of its powers. The Europe of De Gaulle seems to be no more than such a confederation. In other words, he would accept the system of alliances that has existed so often in history when a common danger threatened all (the Holy Alliance against the French Revolution and Napoleon, the 1914–1918 alliance against William II's Germany, or the 1939–1945 alliance against Hitler). Everyone knows how impermanent and revocable these arrangements are. The partisans of the Common Market wanted a permanent organization, a Europe which, little by little, would unify. De Gaulle did not want Europe to unify. At most, he wanted the countries of Europe to consult one another. Yet, in 1961, he proposed a scheme of political co-operation that went a long way toward meeting the objections of his European opponents. His proposal was to bring together, at regular intervals, European heads of state or of government. He suggested a European referendum to get this idea of co-operation accepted by the peoples of the various nations. Then a commission of experts, located in Paris, would prepare the proposals submitted to the conferences of the chiefs of state. He also envisaged a European parliamentary assembly, which would be the common assembly of the European Coal and Steel Community, the Common Market, and Euratom. De Gaulle recognized the existence of those institutions, even though they were tainted by supranationalism.

These suggestions, called the Fouchet Plan, might have been accepted in spite of certain criticisms from Common Market partisans. But, at the beginning of 1962, De Gaulle made an abrupt and very definite *volte-face*. He cut down the part that would be played by the three existing organizations, as well as that of the proposed parliamentary assembly, denying it any powers of action.

After a few seeming concessions to the federal system inaugurated by Robert Schuman, De Gaulle returned to his own concept of a confederation. This his partners could not accept.

The reason for De Gaulle's attitude is mainly one of prestige and national interest. His policy may be anachronistic, but he sticks to it.

He would probably accept a united Europe if it were under French hegemony. Each time that he has seemed to endorse supranational institutions, which imply an organic collaboration between France and its allies, he has done it because he saw an opportunity for his country to play a dominant role.

As soon as he came back to power in 1958, he showed some reservations about NATO. In this military organization under American command, the French contingents lose their autonomy and do not serve France exclusively. On September 24, 1958, De Gaulle sent a memorandum to London and to Washington, suggesting that, within the alliance, Great Britain, the United States, and France take a dominant position and make decisions in common on great political issues. As this preferential treatment was refused by the Anglo-Saxon capitals, De Gaulle removed the Mediterranean French squadron and some French destroyers from NATO. He also refused to allow American stockpiles of nuclear weapons and rocket-launching pads on French soil. At the same time, the French divisions that had returned from Algeria were not put under the Atlantic Command.

Another characteristic example will show how De Gaulle plans a show of European solidarity only when it is to the advantage of France. At Limoges, he disclosed the reason that he finally accepted the Common Market, one of those supranational institutions he dislikes. He said, on May 20, 1962: "We have created an economic community among several countries of Western Europe, which is beginning to bear fruit, and which will be, I believe, especially to France's advantage. Otherwise, we would not have joined it."

The ultimate goal of the General, therefore, seems to be to place a united Europe between the U.S.S.R. and the U.S.A., as he once proclaimed; no longer does he plan to make Europe an example to the world, a viable way of thought and life for our time. He wants only to turn the Common Market to France's profit and to insure that French hegemony, or at least French dominance, will rule all its partners in Europe.

This conception of France's role dates back to Napoleon or to Louis XIV. It shows that, even when he claims to make innovations, De Gaulle is often out of date. Obviously, in the necessary reconstruction of Europe and in the creation of a new political doctrine, France can play a major role. Obviously, because of its tradition of religious and secular humanitarianism, always in search of new and permanent values, France can give new prestige to the quest for liberty in the world: it could dominate by its intellectual and moral authority.

But before France can do this, it must cease to confuse the conspicuous display of material power with the deep realities of spiritual authority. It must also avoid restoring for its own advantage exactly those bankrupt policies which it should replace, if it is to fulfill its mission. It must live in the present and substitute solidarity among the various fatherlands for the selfish nationalism which has provoked so many crises. And De Gaulle, that visionary, must not allow his perspectives to be limited, falsified, and sidetracked by a nostalgia for the past.

THE EVOLUTION OF THE U.S.A. AND THE U.S.S.R.

Of the two conflicting ideologies confronting each other today, the first, the economic liberalism of the Americans and West Europeans, is on the decline, although they continue to see in it a way of life suitable for all countries. To the Americans capitalism is almost an authentic gospel, and they feel it is their vocation to spread it.

The second ideology, Marxian Socialism, has worn thin. In spite of its initial claims to unite the proletariat in all countries, the countries under its totalitarian rule have begun to quarrel seriously (China and the U.S.S.R.) or to drift away (as in the case of Poland, Rumania, and Yugoslavia).

De Gaulle's position toward these two ideologies can be of two kinds. He can take them into account and use them for his own advantage in national politics. Or he can choose, for France and for himself, to evolve a new philosophy adapted to our age. Could Gaullism be the doctrine that supersedes two obsolete systems?

In that case, to insure its survival, it would not be enough for De Gaulle to have the atomic bomb, to manipulate the Constitution and insure his own re-election, or to choose a successor and guarantee the continuation of his regime. These are only expedients. History has shown that once their originator has disappeared, doctrines and the empires which build on them soon come to an end. Nothing remained of Charlemagne's empire, or of Napoleon's, in spite of their steps to make certain of their heirs. Nothing remained of Napoleon III's policy, in spite of the large majority he received in the plebiscite of 1869. De Gaulle's death or removal from the scene would loose such an avalanche of hatred, greed, and avarice that France would risk becoming as divided and as vulnerable as it was when De Gaulle first rescued it. And all the posthumous words of De Gaulle over television would have no more effect than so many other wishes in last wills and testaments. The missing element is a coherent doctrine, the only guarantee for the future, France's whole hope of preserving its dignity and influence on the world scene, and De Gaulle's only chance of not being repudiated as soon as he dies.

This vital problem may crop up during a second seven-year term. The Gaullist regime will either continue to make dramatic innovations from time to time, with its stay in office guaranteed by the General's personality, or it will merely continue to point out all the mistakes or misapprehensions of our decade.

THE IMPASSE OF LIBERALISM

The impasse of liberalism is the impasse of the United States, which causes the Americans a lot of trouble, a great deal of money, even the risk of their children's lives. This great country is our ally and our friend. Without it, we would have ceased long ago to be free men. To escape the injustice of its position, it ought to be more lucid about itself and see the change in its own status in the world.

America is no longer the New World, although it was called that only ten years ago. It has not grown particularly old, but other countries have been born since. The New World is now all those nations which have won independence since the end of the Second World War, all those nations which have won their independence through the processes of change, but which were often underdeveloped, both economically and intellectually, and were not sufficiently prepared for this independence.

The emancipation of the ex-colonies, the creation of these new nations, relegated the United States to the status of an Old World nation. It may be a bit more vigorous than some of the European nations, it may be in less of a rut and more open to new ideas about the future, but nonetheless, that future is linked to memories of a past shared with the Old World, a past that is not acceptable to the new nations.

For these reasons, the Americans are finding it difficult to get along with the new nations. Naïvely, in good faith, and perhaps even generously, the United States after the Second World War tried to use with the new nations the same methods it had used so successfully with the old nations of

Europe after the First World War. Unfortunately, this time it had to deal with countries allergic to both the American concept of liberty and to its economic system. This in large part caused the U.S. trouble in Cuba and South Vietnam.

After the First World War, the Americans wanted to rescue a Europe which had been ruined and decimated by four bloody years of war, and they naturally went about it in the philanthropic manner of good capitalists: they funded loans payable by their European debtors, and allowed credit outlays so that the interest on these debts could be met. In this more or less disinterested manner, America began to finance the Old World, working hand in glove with European firms, sometimes buying them out by the simple and peaceful workings of free enterprise. European governments, on the threshold of bankruptcy and in a period of inflation, were grateful for this aid, although American dollars did not succeed in preventing Spain, Italy, and Germany from becoming dictatorships. But in the European countries that remained free, the capitalist nations lent themselves willingly to American financial operations, and although it was a form of colonization, they did not mind, for this colonization was being practiced in the name of the common god of Freedom.

In the period following the Second World War, American politicians and financiers, recalling their previous success and their tried and true tactics, sought to reapply them, since everyone had been satisfied the first time. With the European countries that were once again in debt and near bankruptcy, their generosity took on an even greater, or at least a perfected, form. After the First World War they had given loans that would, in principle, be repayable some day. But after the Second World War they made loans that would not be repayable, on the condition that those who took them back American policies and use the money chiefly to buy American goods. A well-organized charity always ends by helping the helper. The American peace was a generous and philanthropic one; it helped Europe keep its freedom. At the same time, large units of the American army were sent to guard the Rhine and the Danube, and, as in Korea, the outer limits of the Communist world.

The truth must be acknowledged: if, after the war, Europe did not lose its independence and fall into the camp of the "Popular Democracies," it was because of the United States. Whatever America's ulterior motives, this was a great blessing.

The older countries, accustomed to the mechanics of capitalism and private investment and with the same liberal civilization, took well to United States economic and military aid. But at the same time, the ancient New World was brought into contact with the really new nations, who argued differently and whose point of view was almost completely the opposite.

If you ask a Congolese or a Cuban about freedom he will say he doesn't give a damn. He prefers equality and the independence of which he believes he has been deprived for so long. If you put dollars into his national economy so that it can survive and prosper, he will say that this economy is in the hands of a minority which exploits him. Therefore he is not interested. He would rather have a smaller sum distributed among all, or used to further socialistic enterprises in which he would theoretically be on an equal footing with the rest of the community. He prefers living in *kolkhozes* or *sovkhozes* to dying a free death in front of bank windows that will not open for him. This comes as a great shock to the American who believes in freedom. It is also a great risk for the Free World and for the West, which previously depended on those underdeveloped nations.

These attitudes on the part of the new nations inevitably led to the present decline of the United States' position, and are the reason why its influence in the world is decreasing. No financial or military measures will halt the process.

THE INNER CONTRADICTIONS OF MARXISM

At the same time, we are witnessing the decline of the U.S.S.R., or to be more exact, the decline of the whole Communist world. To analyze the reasons for today's profound division between Russia and China, one must re-examine the origins and the doctrines of Communism, and especially Marx himself. It is Marx, and Marx alone, who enables us to understand what is happening today.

Toward the end of his life, Karl Marx declared to whoever wanted to listen that he was not a Marxist. The political and economic doctrine based on his writings mutilated and paralyzed his ideas. He felt distaste for the rigid and systematic system in which his philosophy was imprisoned. He could not find in that philosophy the successive stages of his intellectual evolution, nor his own variations in dogma nor the fluctuations in his strategy. And he certainly could not find in it his problems of conscience and his inner debates.

Throughout his career, Karl Marx never ceased to waver and contradict himself over the question of dictatorship in relation to nineteenth-century Socialism. That question is still a vital one today. In his early days, before the *Communist Manifesto*, Marx had written a *Critique of Hegel's Political Philosophy* (1841–1842). In it, he took an antistatist and antitotalitarian view, contrasting society, which is the only reality, with the bureaucratic state which oppresses society. "The police, the law courts, and the administration are not the delegates of civil society itself, ruling by the people and for the people's common interest. They are the delegates of the state, given the task of administering the state against civil society."

Certain Socialists of today tend to see "the golden mean" of Marxism in these early works by Marx which do not advocate dictatorship, even the dictatorship of the proletariat.

Closer to dictatorship is the *Communist Manifesto* of 1848 in which Marx advocated state control:

The centralization of credit in the hands of the state, by means of a national bank, with state capital having an exclusive monopoly.
The centralization of all means of transport in the hands of the state.
The increase of nationalized industries and nationalized means of production, the clearing and the improvement of the soil, by means of an overall plan.
The same obligations of work for all, the organization of industrial armies, especially in agriculture.

How fortunate these proposals would be for the dictatorship by a state bureaucracy which Marx had abused so vehemently in the past! What a change of direction for Marx, what a retraction!

It was not his final statement. Marx's vacillations continued. In *The Paris Commune*, written in 1871 under the effect of the sacrifices made by the French Socialists, who were in fact not Marxists, Marx's hostility toward the state returned. He wrote: "The centralized power of the state, with its ever-present organisms, its permanent armies, its police, its bureaucracy, its clergy, and its courts of justice . . . date back to a time of absolute monarch. . . . The Commune's Constitution would have given back to society all the forces absorbed by the state, a parasite which feeds itself on the substance of society and paralyzes its freedom of action. . . ."

Eventually Marx reached a provisional compromise, which he formulated in *A Critique of the Gotha Program*, written in 1875. In it he was able to resolve one serious contradiction in his philosophy, end his wavering, and reconcile the two opposed aspects of his thought. The effects of this compromise can still be felt today. He wrote:

"Between capitalist society and Communist society, there

occurs a period of revolutionary change which transforms the first into the second. There is a period of political transition in which the state can be nothing else than a revolutionary dictatorship of the proletariat."

With these words, the Marxist process was definitively fixed: Marxism would consist of two phases. First, there would be a phase of dictatorship, the dictatorship of the proletariat, during which all power would be wielded either by the Central Party Committee, as in the case of Stalin, or by the Administration. Then would come a phase of easing up. The state would wither away. Without, of course, going back to capitalist free enterprise, the state would grant new freedoms, socialist freedoms, which would not tie men to it so tightly.

Obviously these two phases could not be simultaneous, they had to come in succession. When a country is at the beginning of its Marxist phase, as China is today, it has to apply a strict dictatorship which must be absolutely opposed to bourgeois liberalism. When a country has half a century of Socialist edification behind it, like the U.S.S.R., it can begin to ease up on its dictatorship and allow both itself and its satellites to renew certain ties with liberal countries.

The very outline of Marxism itself, an outline that neither Mao nor Khrushchev nor their successors can ignore, makes for a conflict between Russia and China. It is not merely a conflict between men or between interests, it is not only a clash between two nationalisms, in the normal sense, it is an unavoidable conflict, based on doctrine, between the two periods of Marxism: between its adolescence, which calls for a dictatorship, and its maturity, which implies a return to a certain limited freedom.

DE GAULLE'S HISTORIC ROLE

The decline of American liberalism and of Soviet Marxism, the traces of weakness and the failures in both camps, are not, therefore, the passing phenomena of chance. They are logical and necessary developments which cannot be halted by temporary expedients. On the contrary, they must be taken into account and dealt with. The function of Gaullism and of General de Gaulle may be to do exactly this.

Here Gaullism and De Gaulle must be reconsidered. It is too easy to say that De Gaulle consistently slights England or the United States because he has been slighted by them in the past and because he bears grudges a long time. This may be true, but it is only part of the explanation. If De Gaulle did not feel that American policies were anachronistic, which they unfortunately are, he would act differently. If he felt that America were capable of finding solutions in Cuba or Vietnam or South America which would reconcile the freedom and the Socialist dream necessary to a new people, I am personally convinced that he would forget all his petty grudges. He would then help the United States to fulfill the world mission that it shares with France.

The same is true of his dealings with the Marxist bloc. De Gaulle has no reason to support Communism. He is profoundly religious and could not possibly sympathize with an atheistic ideology. He is obsessed with French independence and inclined to nationalism; therefore he would not ally himself with a political regime that would abolish France's independence were it ever in a position to do so. He does not sympathize with the centralized authority of the Kremlin, which gives orders to the French Communist Party which De Gaulle brands as separatist. He may appear to make advances to a regime which, basically, he opposes utterly, but this is only in order to take advantage of Communist weaknesses or to accentuate them.

Both his temporary estrangement from the United States and his relative *rapprochement* with the Eastern bloc are the result of a precise and profound analysis of the present situation and of the ideological changes in both systems.

This interpretation provides a true insight into the General's action which might otherwise seem contradictory and haphazard. Yet De Gaulle's policy may not be able to produce the grand design the present world dilemma demands.

Confronted by the crumbling of the two antagonistic power blocs, is De Gaulle capable of formulating a coherent doctrine and of pioneering a new civilization? In a word, is he capable of giving the Western democracies, through the leadership of France, new prestige and a new ideal?

The whole question rests there. Sooner or later De Gaulle will appear either as the man who briefly restored a mistaken and antiquated French pseudo-greatness—which would be a catastrophe—or as the inventor of a new political ideology, well suited to his time both in practice and in dogma. If so, history will forget his assaults on French national unity, his lies to fellow Frenchmen, his cruelties, and instead will place him among the greatest of its statesmen whose lasting influence was beneficial not only to his country but to the world.

Postscript, December 12, 1965

One fact is already quite certain. After the election of December 5, De Gaulle can never again be the figure he was before. Even in the best of circumstances, he will never again have the same incontestable authority, nor will he be able to count on a massive majority, as he could in the past. He was not a dictator, as could be clearly seen during the election campaign, but rather a prestigious statesman having at his command an unconditional majority in parliament and a reputedly unanimous support among his countrymen, and he drew the consequences of this in his public actions, where he did as he pleased without referring to anyone else.

Since December 5, all this has changed. De Gaulle no longer represents more than two-fifths of the electoral college. A coalition which was formed to defeat him represents amply more than half the country. From now on he will always have to take the opposition into account, something which he has never known how to do because of his authoritarian nature. Indeed, no French absolute monarch, from Louis XIV through Napoleon to Pétain, ever knew how to get along with an opposition. De Gaulle has lost his momentum and his authority and, no matter what the next years may bring, the extraordinary quality of his adventure has come to an end.

Despite the change in circumstances, I think my analysis of De Gaulle throughout the book remains valid. If De Gaulle no longer has majority support, it is because it is impossible to govern a country like France for a long time while holding her inhabitants as of no account and showing so much indifference toward them. If he has lost his majority, it is also because his policies toward

Europe and his allies were, as we have shown, contrary to the two great traditions which he seems to regard as his own, the Christian tradition and the French tradition. Even when he pursued inevitable and necessary goals, such as giving independence to Algeria, he did so by abusing and deceiving those on whom he depended and who had had confidence in him.

Yet despite his being in the minority and disowned by the French people, De Gaulle will have left ineffaceable marks on French and international political life. He has devised a constitution which can assure the stability of power in the country, after small modifications, and if it is allowed to function normally. He has perceived better than any other European statesman how a reunion of all peoples of ancient Christian civilization, even those temporarily in the agnostic-Communist camp, could come about in the face of the only real menace today, that which comes from Asia. Thus the necessity of rethinking the policies of the free peoples while trying to bring about a *détente* with those who are not free. France without De Gaulle will certainly be very different; without him, perhaps one can say the same of the rest of the world.

On December 5 De Gaulle received more or less forty per cent of the vote. One hopes that in the regime which will succeed him one day at least forty per cent of his ideas will remain.

Index